Praise for

Individuals a...

"In my opinion, this is *the* handbook for ... g for this book since we implemented Agile several ... ss books, the team aspect of Agile has been glossed over in favor of the technical aspects; this book is a welcome change."

—**Sarah Edrie**, Director of Quality Engineering, Harvard Business School

"Cloud Computing, Distributed Architecture, Test Driven Development...these are simple to master compared to building an agile, efficient, and top-performing team. The path from skilled developer/tester to successful manager, team leader, and beyond is now more easily attainable with the insights, knowledge, and guidance provided by Ken Howard and Barry Rogers in *Individuals and Interactions: An Agile Guide*."

—**R.L. Bogetti**, www.RLBogetti.com, Lead System Designer, Baxter Healthcare

"This book provides fantastic insight on how individuals act and relate as a team. Ken and Barry give great examples and exercises to help the reader understand behaviors of each individual and use this knowledge to perform better as a team."

—**Lisa Shoop**, Director Product Development, Sabre-Holdings

"*Individuals and Interactions* is a masterfully crafted must-read for anyone who is serious about understanding and applying the human-centered values of Agile development. It is like Patrick Lencioni meets the Poppendiecks to write 'Agile through the Looking-Glass.' Here the 'Looking-Glass' is the powerful DISC framework, and we see it used to enable different kind of TDD (Team-Driven Development) through the use of stories, examples, models, and guidance."

—**Brad Appleton**, Agile coach/consultant in a Fortune 100 telecom company; coauthor of *Software Configuration Management Patterns*

"This book is essential reading for any engineering team that's serious about Agile development. Its chapters on team dynamics and development lay the foundation for learning all of the factors that enable a team to transform itself into an Agile success story."

—**Bernard Farrell**, Consultant Software Engineer at EMC Corporation

Individuals and Interactions

Individuals and Interactions:

An Agile Guide

**Ken Howard
Barry Rogers**

✦✦Addison-Wesley

Upper Saddle River, NJ • Boston • Indianapolis • San Francisco
New York • Toronto • Montreal • London • Munich • Paris • Madrid
Cape Town • Sydney • Tokyo • Singapore • Mexico City

Many of the designations used by manufacturers and sellers to distinguish their products are claimed as trademarks. Where those designations appear in this book, and the publisher was aware of a trademark claim, the designations have been printed with initial capital letters or in all capitals.

The authors and publisher have taken care in the preparation of this book, but make no expressed or implied warranty of any kind and assume no responsibility for errors or omissions. No liability is assumed for incidental or consequential damages in connection with or arising out of the use of the information or programs contained herein.

The publisher offers excellent discounts on this book when ordered in quantity for bulk purchases or special sales, which may include electronic versions and/or custom covers and content particular to your business, training goals, marketing focus, and branding interests. For more information, please contact:

U.S. Corporate and Government Sales
(800) 382-3419
corpsales@pearsontechgroup.com

For sales outside the United States please contact:

International Sales
international@pearson.com

Visit us on the Web: informit.com/aw

Library of Congress Cataloging-in-Publication Data
Howard, Ken, 1962-
 Individuals and interactions : an agile guide / Ken Howard, Barry Rogers.
  p. cm.
  Includes bibliographical references and index.
  ISBN 978-0-321-71409-1 (pbk. : alk. paper) 1. Teams in the workplace. 2. Communication. I. Rogers, Barry, 1963- II. Title.
  HD66.H695 2011
  658.4'022--dc22
                          2011001898

Text printed in the United States on recycled paper at RR. Donnelley and Sons, Crawfordsville, Indiana.

First printing April 2011
ISBN-13: 978-0-321-71409-1
ISBN-10: 0-321-71409-1

Writing a book like this cannot be done alone.
It requires a tremendous amount of knowledge, skills,
experience, and support. I dedicate this book to those
who supported me throughout this process:
My family—Mom & Dad, Kacy, Joe, Sean, TJ, Danni,
Nikki; each never doubted I would get this done.
Armand Garcia shared his extensive expertise
in psychology, which helped me understand why
we humans behave the way we do.
Finally, to my colleagues at Improving Enterprises:
Thanks for teaching me through your demonstration
of how individuals can interact productively,
and reminding me that we are a work in progress,
always improving.

—Ken Howard

I dedicate this book to my darling,
"high S" wife, Jane. Thanks for all your support
throughout my career. I also dedicate it to my two
beautiful daughters, Alicia and Nicole ("DI" and
"SC," respectively). I love you all. I thank Dr. Abelson
for his wisdom and feedback regarding the DISC
content in the book. I also thank my good friend,
partner, and CEO, Curtis Hite for his encouragement
to everyone at Improving Enterprises to broaden our
reaches in helping the software community.
I appreciate your support as well as your friendship.

—Barry Rogers

Contents

Preface

The Agile Manifesto resulted after that legendary group of individuals met at a Utah ski resort in February, 2001.

It's ironic that despite buy-in and adoption of the manifesto, most of what has been published, spoken about, and even practiced are things from the right half of the manifesto. You have probably used many of the common agile-related items such as Scrum, user stories, eXtreme Programming, test-driven development, product backlogs, task boards, and the list goes on and on. At a high level, the majority of these are either processes or tools. Yet the Agile Manifesto espouses individuals and interactions over processes and tools.

So, why is there so much focus on process and tools? Because they are all enablers of the values depicted in the Agile Manifesto. For example, if you maintain a product backlog as part of the Scrum process, you have a prioritized list of features, and every four weeks (or whatever your iteration cycle is) you develop potentially shippable code. At the end of each iteration, the product owner helps the development team determine what they will develop next. You can easily see that these items enable "responding to change over following a plan"; "working software over comprehensive documentation" and "customer collaboration over contract negotiation."

The one value that does not get as much attention is "individuals and interactions over processes and tools." One reason for this is because the majority of individuals in our industry started out in college as computer SCIENCE or software ENGINEERING students. Yet individuals and interactions focus more on psychology and human behavior. It is less black and white and less perfect. Arguably the most common and most complex issue companies and project teams typically face is related to human behavior and communication.

In one of the first popular agile books, *Agile Software Development*, Alistair Cockburn introduced us to agile with an excellent discussion of the human side of developing software. He addressed culture, communication, cooperation, and other "soft" subjects that are at the core of agile. Since that book was published in 2002, there has been sparse coverage.

This book is not intended to take you on a philosophical journey. Instead, it is structured as a user's guide. Practical information is presented that is relevant to the issues that project teams tend to encounter, with stories, tips, and best practices that can be put into action. In addition, facilitator instructions are included with valuable exercises that you can administer with your team or that can be combined as part of a comprehensive team dynamics workshop.

How to Use This Book

This book is written as a user's guide to optimizing individuals and interactions on an agile project. Your use of this book may vary based on your role.

If you are a manager, ScrumMaster, or product owner, or play some other leadership role, you may want to make two passes through the book: First, read the chapters to gain a better understanding of your team and why it behaves the way it does. Second, choose activities described in the book and facilitate exercises with your team to improve.

If you are a consultant tasked with helping teams succeed, identify areas needing the most attention and select content and exercises that address those areas. It can be useful to facilitate reading groups (for example, lunch and learn book reviews) where the team reads and discusses one chapter at a time.

> **Resource**
>
> When you see the book icon, look for a reference to a resource that you can dive into for deeper coverage of a topic being discussed. Rather than having to scour through a bibliography at the end of the book, look for sources of great material presented alongside the topics it supports.

If you are a trainer, the book has been designed to provide the ingredients you need to facilitate an Agile Team Dynamics workshop. Instructions for conducting the workshop are described in Chapter 9, "Team Dynamics Workshop."

Lastly, most readers of this book are members of project teams. Some work on agile projects, some may be considering agile, and others have not had the opportunity to work on agile projects. The knowledge and exercises in this book are not exclusive to agile project teams. Understanding behavior and social factors on any project team is the first step to building a cohesive, productive team.

Lastly, most readers of this book are members of project teams. Some work on agile projects, some may be considering agile, and others have not had the opportunity to work on agile projects. The knowledge and exercises in this book are not exclusive to agile project teams. Understanding behavior and social factors on any project team is the first step to building a cohesive, productive team.

About the Authors

Ken Howard works at Improving Enterprises, where he specializes in helping companies increase productivity through efficient practices and pragmatic organizational dynamics. Ken has been involved in most aspects of software development for more than 26 years with such languages as diverse as COBOL, Smalltalk, and Java. Over the years Ken has provided consulting, training, and mentoring to companies in 12 countries around the world, helping with adoption of software development best practices. He eagerly embraced the opportunity to share many of the things he has learned with a broader audience through the publication of this book.

Barry Rogers is President of Improving Enterprises, Dallas, Texas. He is an accomplished Certified ScrumMaster and Certified Scrum Practitioner. Barry supports clients in both a hands-on and mentorship/coaching capacity, helping teams adopt agile/Scrum and improve human dynamics. Barry is a Speaker and also facilitates leadership, agile, and project management training sessions.

Introduction

There have been countless books on the subject of human behavior and communication. Psychologists, sociologists, organizational behavior experts, and others have conducted studies, published journal articles, taught courses, and granted degrees in this subject area.

Sidebar

Throughout the book you'll find complementary stories, tips, best practices, and resources. As you read through the primary content of the book, don't forget to take a look at these for additional valuable information.

So why another book on this well-covered topic? This book is the first of its kind—the first to address individuals and interactions on an agile software project. The illustrations, examples, and exercises are all specifically tailored to address the needs of an agile team. The Agile Manifesto begins with valuing individuals and interactions over processes and tools. Despite that, most that has been written, taught, and implemented for the agile community focuses on processes and tools. This book offers a refreshing change—the entire book is dedicated to individuals and their interactions on an agile project.

A Brief History of Organizational Behavior

The sociology of a company is a fascinating thing to observe. Over the past 100 years, organizational behavior has been researched (often empirically and sometimes scientifically), written about, studied, learned, transformed, applauded, and criticized. Courses on organizational behavior are required in most (if not all) college business degree programs, so most college educated managers have at least a cursory understanding of the evolution of corporate societies.

It may seem odd to attach the term sociology with an organization, yet it's fitting. Organizations contain societal elements such as culture, laws (policies), class (pecking order), structure, language, and so on. Although countless books have been written about this subject, there are just a few key notable milestones in the evolution of organizational behavior. This field of study is broad and deep, and to better understand it, it could be sliced and diced a variety of ways. As you begin to explore the dynamics of a team through individuals and their interactions with one another, look at the following four pivotal evolutionary stages of the maturity of organizational behavior.

Stage 1: People Are Machines (Late 1800s–Mid 1900s)

In the early 1900s Frederick Taylor became one of the first efficiency experts. He developed an approach to optimizing efficiency in organizations that was later referred to as Scientific Management. Taylor's principles of management were based on the premise that workers can't be trusted to be productive on their own. Taylor felt that workers limit their productivity due to the fear that if they maximize productivity, they will run out of work and lose their jobs. Taylor's solution was to study their work methods carefully and to develop highly prescriptive optimized processes that must be followed by all workers.

Franklin and Lillian Gilbreth were also efficiency experts whose expertise was time and motion studies of individuals. The Gilbreths would study the movements of individuals in a factory and relocate people and machines to strike an optimal balance between energy exerted to output delivered. The Gilbreths later gained some notoriety when some of their children wrote two books about life at home. The most popular of these books was titled *Cheaper by the Dozen*. The Gilbreths had twelve children, and they operated their household in the same efficient manner as the factories where they worked.

Franklin Gilbreth put language records in the bathroom so that otherwise inefficient time could be spent in a productive activity. Probably the most outrageous story referred to the time when one of the children got a case of tonsillitis. When consulting with the doctor and discovering how much time would be required to deal with removal of this one child's tonsils, Gilbreth extrapolated how much time would be later required if he had to repeat this exercise eleven more times. Instead, he brought the doctor to the house and removed the tonsils from all twelve kids at once!

The approach used by Taylor and the Gilbreths defined an era that overlooked the *humanness* of human beings. Humans were just cogs in a machine. This may have looked good on the balance sheet, but it was not a sustainable way to treat people in the workplace.

Stage 2: People Are Emotional Beings (1940s–1970s)

In 1955, a factory in Illinois called Hawthorne Works became the location where a pivotal change was made in how organizational behavior was perceived. Brightness of lighting at the factory was adjusted upward and downward to determine the effect on worker productivity. The study demonstrated that productivity increased not as a result of brighter or dimmer light, but as a result of change. This was reinforced as other superficial changes to the workplace were made, also increasing productivity. The Hawthorne study showed that workers increase productivity when interest is shown in them. The Hawthorne study led to a new field of interest in business—addressing the emotional needs of workers.

During this period, Douglas McGregor described the contrast between Theory X and Theory Y managers. Theory X managers presume that employees will not work unless they are motivated to work. They often believe that money is the only way to motivate an employee and that employees must be ruled with an iron fist. Theory Y managers, on the other hand, believe that employees want to perform well at work and that in the right setting, employees will be self-motivated and productive workers.

McGregor's work was based on another important theory introduced in the same timeframe, Maslow's hierarchy of needs. Maslow explains how behavior is a function of our physiological needs and our need for safety, love, and belonging, esteem, and self-actualization. Later in this book, Maslow's hierarchy of needs is offered with guidance on how to address common needs conflicts that often arise on agile project teams.

Another important contribution during this period was the psychological inventory. A popular inventory mechanism was called DISC, which analyzed and described an individual's behavior in a specific setting. DISC is used throughout the book to aid in explaining why people behave the way they do.

Stage 3: Organization Is a Machine (1980s–2000s)

In the late 1980s, many companies were inspired to raise their competitive edge. The expression "We must beat the 800-pound gorilla" was used liberally, referring to the huge companies that seemed to be successful despite themselves. Smaller companies saw an opportunity to operate leaner, faster, smarter, and with more agility than the huge companies.

MIT computer science professor Michael Hammer introduced the world to Business Process Reengineering (BPR) in 1990. BPR initiatives were rampant in many companies in the early 1990s as they strove to drive waste out of everything they did. Every procedure, job function, and task was analyzed to the nth degree to assess which added no value and could be removed. The BPR wave lost favor with many because the original intent was lost with the BPR process itself. BPR was properly focused on improvement and increased efficiency, but the way BPR initiatives were executed was highly inefficient and costly. These huge analyses efforts dragged on with reams of published findings but little action. Many unqualified BPR consulting firms attached themselves to the popular label but failed to deliver the desired results. As a result, BPR became a distasteful topic to executives at many companies.

Another MIT professor, Peter Senge, introduced the concept of the *learning organization* during this period. Senge presented a framework for a company to continuously improve by never resting on its laurels and to learn and adapt with every move it makes. Senge's model was far more abstract than Hammer's, making it more challenging for unqualified consulting firms to appropriately emulate. The learning organization required a cultural shift from the bottom up and from the top down.

The work of Hammer, Senge, and many others during this 20–30 year period framed a significant transformation period for businesses. The business itself was treated as an organism that could sustain order of magnitude improvement. Much like an overweight, out-of-shape person can improve health through diet and exercise, an organization could do the same thing. Staying with that analogy, the unhealthy person may have gotten that way through years of ignorance and neglect. Employing a personal trainer and dietician to coach and guide may be necessary for positive change to occur. An unhealthy company cannot tweak a few things here and there and expect significant improvement. The works of this period caused organizations to recognize this.

Stage 4: Empowered Teams Transform the Organization (Current Trend)

With a foundation of understanding that people provide the muscle and intelligence of an organization and that an organization cannot exist without people, the current trends in organizational behavior emphasize the power of the people. People are not in an organization, people *are* the organization. Therefore, people ought to avoid doing silly, wasteful things. Taking away all constraints and restraints, people with the proper environment, knowledge, and skills will likely approach a project pragmatically and sensibly.

Empowering skilled people to enable their own capabilities and work together productively requires an environment of trust. This trusting environment is rare, yet it is a mandatory prerequisite to successful employment of agility. This book offers some motivation for moving to an agile environment, but it places far more emphasis on the knowledge and skills needed to employ agility with ease and success.

Birds of a Feather...

What causes a flock of birds to move in a coordinated orchestrated fashion? How is the leader selected, and how does the huge flock navigate changes in direction so swiftly and smoothly that it appears to happen instantaneously? This is one of the great mysteries of nature.

Depending on the circumstances, some humans are inclined to lead and others to follow. Some may lead in some situations and follow in others. Some strive to always lead, whereas others may strive to always follow. Through the years, scientists and scholars have tried to explain individual and group behavior. Some of these theories have tried to explain what is, whereas others have tried to define what could be.

Regardless of what some author chooses to write about, humans are what they have always been. Some will lead, some will follow, some will conform, and some will resist. The complexities of putting more than one person together can be the source of friction, while at the same time it can be the spark that inspires great advancements. This book explores the dynamics of the singular individual and the dynamics of groups of individuals.

PART I

Individuals and
Interactions

Chapter 1

Autonomous Securities, LLC

Nathan Patterson walked out of his annual retrospective meeting with a great feeling. Sure, the bonus he knows he will see in his next paycheck is nice, especially in today's economy. But what made him feel even better was the amazing sense of accomplishment he felt turning around his once underperforming organization. It was this time last year that his job was on the line. What had happened in the course of the past year that made things so drastically different?

At last year's retrospective, Nathan's group had missed all project completion milestones at Autonomous Securities. What puzzled Nathan was that he personally hired the entire team and, without a doubt in his mind, knew that his employees were top-notch based on all the technical interviews and tests he administered. Nathan contemplated all the project artifacts and history of events and hypothesized that the workers were simply not executing at their full potential. So why was this amazing group of people that Nathan assembled not performing up to his expectations?

At the conclusion of last year's meeting, at the end of his rope, Nathan had decided to seek outside help and hired Lydia Stewart, a consultant specializing in increasing team efficiency. "I do not understand why we are not meeting schedules. I assembled the perfect team, and I am using agile processes," Nathan explained to Lydia. Lydia immediately thought to herself that it was a yellow flag when Nathan referred to agile as a process instead of a set of values.

After observing Nathan's team in action, it was evident to Lydia that the team was not behaving as a team but as a group of individuals. She explained to Nathan that the social factors in the workplace presented tremendous challenges to worker productivity—more than any other factor. Team dynamics, individual behavioral differences, motivators, leadership styles, and numerous other factors greatly affect productivity.

This book tells the story of how Lydia helped Nathan transform his team into what it is today. The goal of this book is to help you, the reader, better understand how and why individuals behave the way they do when working on a team. Through this transformation there is a point where you may come to differentiate the importance of personal success versus the success of your team. This book provides specific, detailed approaches and exercises that you can use to help your team perform as a team.

Chapter 2

Behavior and Individuals

During her first week, Lydia decided to sit back and simply observe communication between members of the team. She first attended a meeting where the team was discussing the design of the system.

Lydia noticed that Sean was dominating most of the conversations. As a result, most of his ideas were the ones that defined the design. Carl and Lisa contributed to the discussion and seemed to be having fun. David, who was the most experienced developer in the group, was overpowered by the conversations and could not seem to get a word in edgewise. So he did not offer too much assistance to the meeting. Eric seemed quite uncomfortable when Sean put him on the spot asking his opinion on the maintainability of the design. Ravi wanted to get into some of the details behind design decisions to feel comfortable that they would work, but Sean seemed to want to drive things fairly quickly.

By the end of the meeting, you could sense a bit of tension among members of the team, and although they walked away with a design, Lydia could tell not everyone felt comfortable with the approach. The bigger issue was not the design, however, but that the team was not acting like a team. Some key opinions were never spoken. And individuals were getting frustrated with one another.

Lydia knew her first step to increasing the team's performance was to get the team to start understanding each other's behaviors and to modify their communication styles to work more effectively as a team.

Communication Framework

If you ask people to define *agile*, you will probably get as many different answers as the number of people you ask. To make it simpler, what if you ask them to abstract the top three definitions in just one or two words? Most would include the words "communication" or "teamwork" in their definitions.

The Agile Manifesto indicates, "Individuals and Interactions over Process and Tools," and one of the Agile principles states, "The most efficient and effective method of conveying information to and within a development team is face-to-face conversation." So, if agile is, to a large degree, about increasing communication effectiveness and the way teams work together, why would anyone begin an agile project without first establishing a communication framework that fosters better communication and teamwork?

Resource
http://Agilemanifesto.org.

Have you ever heard of project teams that successfully start an agile endeavor with much excitement and enthusiasm, but over time, the project falls apart? It is similar to building a house on a sink hole. It appears great at the onset. But after a period of time and when you apply some pressure and stress, the house sinks. To help prevent sink holes on your projects, this chapter discusses a valuable framework for enabling better communication: the history, definition, and importance of this framework are covered.

DISC History

The framework discussed in this chapter is called DISC. You may have already heard of DISC because it has been around much longer than agile and even longer than Lean whose roots date back to the 1930s when Toyota moved from a spinning and weaving company to a car company. You could tie the history of DISC all the way back to 400 B.C. when Hippocrates observed humans and classified four different behaviors.

In 1928, Dr. William Moulton Marston published a book titled, *The Emotions of Normal People*, in which he described the DISC theory. Over the years, several companies have provided statistical validation and continuous improvements to DISC.

So DISC has been around for a while. But it is only a relatively recent development that it is being applied to achieve greater communication on agile teams. Even though I had been using DISC on my software project teams for many years prior, I had initially heard of the association of DISC with enabling success on agile projects during my Certified ScrumMaster training by Craig Larman in 2006.

DISC Definition

You can think of DISC as a behavioral fingerprint. Everyone's behavior contains a blend of four elements, but no two people's blends are exactly alike. It is this blend that drives how individuals behave. To begin to gain an understanding of DISC, it is easiest to simplify it in terms of one's dominant behavior. That is, if someone's dominant behavior is a D (with secondary I), you may simply refer to that person's behavior as a DI. This dominant behavior explains how people will behave and communicate. So what do these letters mean?

The D—Dominator

D's have a need to accomplish. They are decisive, thrive on challenges, exercise authority, and hold themselves in high regard. D's have a tendency to deal straightforwardly with people and may interrupt you in mid-sentence. They may be perceived by others as being arrogant, opinionated, or rude. The higher the D, the more intense these behaviors. It should come as no surprise that many CEOs of companies are D's.

The I—Influencer

I's have a need to trust and talk. They trust, accept, and like others. I's enjoy talking and are animated (for example, they tend to talk with their hands or full facial expressions), persuasive, and optimistic. I's may have a tendency to become emotional or excitable and may be a poor judge of character because they give people the benefit of the doubt. I's usually see the glass as half full. I's typically make the best communicators.

The S—Supporter

S's have a need to support others. They are good team players, avoid attention, have good listening skills, and are deliberate or self-sacrificing. S's typically build close relationships with a relatively small group of friends. High S's may not make the smallest decisions. You might walk all over high S's as long as they feel appreciated. S's tend to make the best team players.

The C—Critical Thinker

C's have a need for perfection and quality. They aim for accuracy—and have a capacity for and enjoy concentrating on details. C's think systematically and are problem solvers. They are typically serious, intense, thorough, and cautious at decision making. C's tend to set high standards for themselves that are above the norm. They may become critical of others if they do not meet their high standards. C's typically see the glass as half empty because they want things to be perfect. Our industry is dominated by high C's who are computer "scientists" or software "engineers." Coding, testing, designing, and capturing requirements all take analytic skills and close attention to details.

A Funny Story

Once upon a time four coworkers, each with a different dominant behavioral profile, got on an elevator.

The D immediately kept pressing the close button, quickly getting annoyed that for some reason it was not closing, but kept pressing the button over and over and over.

The reason the elevator was not closing was because the I kept inviting more people into the elevator.

The S stood quietly in the back corner concerned that the elevator doors might close and hurt someone.

The C was also in the back corner looking worried. He was staring at the maximum weight capacity sign in the elevator and calculating in his head the weight of each passenger as they entered.

So Why Is This Important?

The next few sections answer this question, including understanding and accepting others, the need to communicate in your own language, and the language of DISC. There is also a section regarding strategies for communicating with others depending on your behavioral profile.

Understanding and Accepting Others

Individuals that understand DISC can perform better on teams by understanding and accepting other team member's behaviors.

The following story is a real-world example of an event that occurred at a consulting company several years ago. Marcia, the recruiter, was a high D, and John, one of the principal consultants in the company, was a high C. Marcia was frustrated. "I just want a simple answer whether we should hire a candidate that John just finished interviewing, and John said he would need to think about it overnight and get back with me tomorrow," she said. "I do not understand why I can't get a simple answer right away. We are under the gun to move quickly." At the same time, John was equally annoyed at Marcia for being so "pushy," wanting an immediate answer.

The next day, John provided a long, involved, and detailed write-up describing the candidate interview. John described the elevator simulation problem he had given the candidate. He went on to describe the candidate's answers in great detail, including the candidate's ability to use abstraction and design patterns. The detailed write-up went on to describe John's analysis of these answers and depicted the pros/cons of the candidate's solution. Finally, John recommended hiring the candidate. Although frustrated that it took so long, Marcia was happy to get a bottom-line answer. She did not actually care about the detailed response but was happy to see a conclusive and positive answer and made an offer to the candidate.

Several months later, both Marcia and John took the DISC assessments and were in a room discussing the results. Both laughed out loud as they immediately reflected on this event. Both Marcia and John understood why they behaved the way they did and realized they could better accept and communicate with one another now that they realized why. From that point forward, Marcia tried to be a little less pushy and give John time to do his analysis to make a decision. And John tried his best to provide a quicker answer. But most important, they understood and more readily accepted one another.

Communicate in Your Own Language

Another reason DISC is so important is because people have a need to communicate in their own language. Although you cannot permanently change your behavioral profile, you can adapt your behavior and communication style to not induce stress on a person with whom you are communicating.

Say, for example, that you were giving a presentation to a leader of a company regarding how much a particular project will cost. How would you modify your presentation if you were presenting to a high D? To a high C?

If you are presenting to a high D, you should give an executive summary first indicating the bottom line of how much the project will cost. Then get into the facts—and be open to skipping some of the details. Otherwise the person will flip to the end of his hardcopy version of your slides (if he has a hardcopy version and may become frustrated if he does not), wanting to know the bottom line.

When presenting to a high C, you should do the opposite. Present all the facts first, followed by the price, perhaps with some type of a traceability matrix back to all the details. Otherwise, the person will feel uncomfortable being hit with numbers without first knowing the supporting data that led you to your conclusion.

The following is another example of a real-world situation. A group had just finished DISC training and were checking into a hotel. There were two clerks at the hotel front desk. One checked in with the first clerk who smiled and asked, "Where are you from? How was your trip?" Another checked in with the second clerk who did not smile, got straight down to business, and asked, "What type of credit card will you be using?"

To an I traveler, the first clerk would appear to be warm, and the second clerk would be a bit of a "jerk." To a D traveler, the first clerk would be quite annoying and would be wasting time especially considering he is tired and just trying to check into his room. The second clerk would be perceived by the D as being efficient. If the hotel owner knew about DISC, think about how she could potentially increase her guest satisfaction by teaching her clerks how to greet guests based on their body language and communication when walking into the lobby?

The Language of DISC

The final reason that DISC is important is because it enables people to leverage "the language of DISC."

If everyone has been trained on DISC, it makes for a great and sometimes necessary ice breaker. The following is a real-world example depicting the language of the DISC. This story is about a company in which the CEO was, you guessed it, a high D. The CEO was actually a high DI. When a high D is also an equally high I, that person tends to be seen as charismatic.

There would periodically be times where a group would get together to brainstorm ideas. The CEO would naturally dominate the conversation. He was smart and had a lot of good ideas. But so did others. When the group could not get a word in edgewise, one of them could say to the CEO something like, "Your D is acting up right now." He knew he was a high D, so he would laugh, and others would get a chance to talk. Without the "language of DISC," it would be difficult to essentially ask him to kindly shut up. When using the language of DISC, people generally laugh and get the point.

The following is yet another true story. A new project was kicked off with about 20 people in a room—a mix of business stakeholders and project team members. In typical fashion, one of the lead business stakeholders was an extremely high D, whereas one of the senior developers was an extremely high C.

The senior developer made a suggestion to which the main business stakeholder said, "Do you know what your specific role is going to be on the project?" The senior developer did not know how to respond and simply said, "No not exactly." Of course, on an agile project, there are only three roles (that is, Product Owner, ScrumMaster, and team member), but the business stakeholder did not know that. The business stakeholder actually replied, "Then I do not want to listen to your suggestions." It was an awkward moment, and the room was silent for what appeared to be 10 minutes. (Although it was only about 10 seconds.) It ruined their relationship, and it was a shame the team was not trained in DISC prior to this initial meeting. Anyone could have easily broken the ice with the language of DISC. It would have taken care of an awkward moment by breaking the silence, and most likely the business stakeholder would have apologized, salvaging that relationship. You can see how the cost of not executing a DISC group session can be costly to a project because relationships can be permanently severed.

Strategies for Communicating

Table 2.1 provides a brief overview of strategies for communicating with others depending on their behavioral profiles.

Table 2.1 *Strategies for Communicating*

Behavior	Strategies for Communicating
D	Get to the point; be clear; be specific; be brief; present an overview with facts; provide alternatives; and talk about results.
I	Be friendly; talk; ask questions; stay on the topic; be open; talk feelings; and have fun.
S	Allow time to warm up; be part of a team; present new ideas gently; be agreeable; suggest outcomes; and draw out their opinions.
C	Be serious; be prepared; be organized; present details; present pros and cons; give solid evidence; allow time for questions; ask questions; and give options for decisions.

How Do You Take a DISC Assessment?

One of the beauties of DISC is its simplicity. If you get good at it, you can often tell a person's behavioral profile just by observing body language combined with the way the person communicates. Masters of DISC will often not need assessments at all. However, certain elements of a good DISC provider's product are not known just by observing and communicating.

Notice the words, "A good DISC provider's product." There are plenty of DISC providers if you Google it. However, they are not all equal. First, you should select one that analyzes and provides information using all behavioral elements and not one that simply provides a DISC graph (see Figure 2.1). To interpret the graph, an individual's dominant behaviors are depicted by the elements above the bolded midline. For example, in this graph, the individual's behavioral profile would be a CS. Many companies provide powerful and amazingly accurate reports full of useful information regarding an individual's behavioral characteristics including sections describing the person, how to or not to communicate with them, and how they will behave under stress.

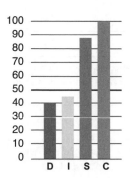

Figure 2.1 *DISC graph*

Finally, it is highly recommended to choose a DISC provider that provides a "wheel," which is discussed in Chapter 6, "Behavior and Teams." This is critical because it applies to the dynamics of a team and not just the behaviors of an individual. If you obtain a DISC report without getting a wheel, you are getting only partial benefit.

The Appendix in this book contains a free DISC assessment. Although the free assessment does not produce detailed reports or a wheel, it can get you started by providing your DISC graphs.

Closing

Many would agree that the greatest challenge on software projects is not technology, not the schedule, not requirements, but is people-related. The larger the team, the more potential for conflict. It is well worth the effort at the onset of every project to establish a framework for communication and to provide insight into the behavioral aspects of each of the team members.

It is easy to fall into the trap of organizing a big DISC event where everybody takes their DISC assessment, discusses it, and then puts it on the shelf to gather dust. The true benefit of doing DISC individually and as a team is to incorporate the awareness of DISC into your daily interactions. Accepting others, modifying your communication style, and using the language of DISC are all important. Because teams evolve and some individuals will adapt their behaviors to changing work environments, many teams find it helpful to periodically revisit the DISC.

Chapter 3

───

Team Dynamics

It was Monday morning, and Lydia was excited to observe the team's sprint planning meeting. When she entered the room, the team was already assembled around the task board actively discussing the project's user stories. People were smiling and listening intently. At first glance, all seemed good with this picture. Then as Lydia joined the group and watched for a while, she witnessed something she had never seen before on an agile team. Sean was at the task board assigning tasks to all members of the team. From Lydia's observations of Sean last Friday (see Chapter 2, "Behavior and Individuals"), she knew Sean's behavior was a very high D; therefore he tended to be outspoken and drive things perhaps a little more than he should. However, this issue was much deeper than communication style. Lydia knew that as a ScrumMaster, Sean should be more of a facilitator than a dictator. He was not allowing the team to self-organize.

This chapter explains what self-organization means and why self-organization is critical to optimize a team's performance.

───

An Apoplectic Dilemma

When Apollo 13 was headed toward the Moon on April 13, 1970, nobody had planned for how to handle the explosion of an oxygen tank on board. The project to build the spaceship had been meticulously planned and executed. Every step, every task was carefully and thoughtfully carried out. There were countless people involved in the project, and everyone performed the role they were hired to do. The NASA project culture was extremely structured and chock-full of predictability.

When flight controllers heard Commander Lovell say, "Houston, we've had a problem," all prescriptive processes, defined roles, and project protocol were quickly forgotten. There was no time to prepare timelines and draw Gantt Charts. Solution proposals were not solely the responsibility of those with the proper engineering credentials. Experts rallied together to perform emergency innovation, which resulted in a creative solution that safely returned the crew to Earth by converting the Lunar Module into a space "lifeboat." This extreme situation may not be indicative of a typical project setting; however, it is a clear illustration of a team self-organizing to accomplish a goal.

A Different Approach to Teams

In 1986, Takeuchi and Nonaka introduced an approach to product development teams that was analogous to the sport of rugby. The emphasis was on a team as a singular, holistic unit. Citing examples of successful product development projects at several companies, projects were initiated when senior management kicked off the process with a stretch goal—an extreme target that would raise the adrenaline of the team and bind them together with a singular focus on achieving the goal.

Resource

The New New Product Development Game,
Hirtaka Takeuichi and Ikujuir Nonaka.
Harvard Business Review, 1986.

The stretch goal instilled a tension-filled atmosphere that could be a time bomb if mixed with traditional organizational structures, roles, processes, and expectations. Other changes were necessary.

Self-organizing project teams operate in an entrepreneurial manner. Prior expectations of individuals on the team performing prescribed roles are abandoned. The problem to be solved becomes the center of the team's attention, and the urgency of solving that problem together causes the team to self-organize and find its optimal state.

For self-organizing to work, three conditions must be present:

- **Empowerment:** Top management specifies the goal, funds the effort, sets boundaries, and is responsive to the team when approached for support. Otherwise, the team is left to operate and make decisions within the boundaries of the project.

- **Continuous improvement:** Simply put, the team continuously raises the bar and works together to reach that bar. The team improves together as a holistic unit and shares in the satisfaction of becoming better. Through the process each team member's strengths will be revealed, and they will reach out to one another to leverage one another's strengths when needed.

The "bar" is not just related to individual skills. It also refers to busting through conventional business and societal expectations. Conventional wisdom can constrain the field of possible solutions to problems, and a self-transcendent team doesn't allow those barriers to limit its capabilities.

- **Multifunctional teams:** Self-organizing teams require abandonment of the conventional "relay race" where one functional group completes a task and hands its deliverables to the next group that performs tasks related to its specialty. Instead, all specialties required of a project are combined into one cohesive team. Multifunctional teams are key to accelerating the progress of the project. For example, multifunctional teams could include experts in sales, marketing, design, engineering, and quality assurance.

In addition to specialized skills, cross-fertilization not only refers to behavioral diversity, but there is also added value in combining team members with different complementary behavioral profiles. See Chapter 2 for a description of behavioral profiles.

Capitalizing on Strengths

In his popular book *Now, Discover Your Strengths*, Marcus Buckingham discusses a Gallup poll that found that only a small percentage of people surveyed believe that their jobs enable them to work on tasks that leverage what they do best.

Resource

Now, Discover Your Strengths, Marcus Buckingham and Donald O. Clifton, Simon and Schuster, 2001.

It may be possible to drive a screw into a piece of wood using a hammer, and it may be possible to use a screwdriver to drive a nail. Common sense indicates that it would make better sense to use the hammer to drive the nail and use the screwdriver with the screw. But what if you have a screw and a nail and only a hammer? It's common to be handed a problem and not have access to an optimal set of resources. The logical solution in this case would be to get your hands on a screwdriver, even if you don't have one in your toolbox.

On projects, though, individuals are often asked to perform tasks that they are not qualified to do. This can happen when project plans are meticulously laid out that marry tasks with available resources. A high-performing team would recognize strength-task mismatches and take corrective action. That could include shuffling assignments around, or it could mean reaching outside the team to leverage skills that don't exist on the team.

At face value, this approach could potentially discourage employee development and growth. When there is a goal to develop and expand the skills of a team member, it's important for that goal to be stated and completely transparent. When a high-performing team adopts a shared goal to help Fred improve his design skills, Fred's progress can be accelerated through the encouragement and support of the team. Recognize that when employee growth becomes part of a project's charter, it can consume resources and time that cannot be spent on other project goals.

So again, high-performing, self-transcendent teams are skillful at leveraging each individual's seminal strengths. Additionally, these teams can recognize skill gaps and work rigorously to fill them.

The Anarchical Team

When considering self-organizing teams, it's possible that management may fear anarchy. In the novel *Lord of the Flies*, when a group of boys are stranded on an island with no adults, they are forced to self-organize to survive. In this situation, self-organization is not reliable on its own. Although some of the boys were focused on doing what was necessary for survival and the rescue, others were focused solely on individual needs. Eventually, individuality led to irrational primal and savage behavior, which overpowered efforts by the few focused on survival.

Resource
Lord of the Flies, William Golding, Capricorn Books, 1954.

When individual needs take precedence over the needs of the overall group, an environment similar to anarchy (lack of government) can occur—a.k.a., "Every man for himself." In this situation, goals in the best interest of the group overall are not likely to be met. But who decides what is in the best interest of the group overall? Should those values and overarching naturally reveal themselves, or should some representative of authority prescribe them?

The Evolution of a Maturing Team

When a new team is formed, a natural maturing process occurs. Tuckman described the evolution of a team in four stages:

- **Forming**

  - Members get to know each other.

  - Participants agree on goals and begin completing tasks.

  - Individuals seek to understand each others' skills and behavioral tendencies.

  - Emphasis of team members tends to be on individual needs.

  - Strong direct leadership is typical at this stage.

- **Storming**

  - Divergent ideas are raised, which can lead to conflict.

  - Group goals from the Forming stage may be questioned.

  - Individuals from some behavioral profiles suffer through this stage, [whereas] others enjoy the drama.

  - Strong leadership is necessary to pass from this stage to the next.

- **Norming**

  - Give and take occurs between team members.

  - Individuals adapt their behavior and start to focus on accomplishing team goals rather than individual goals.

  - In this stage, it's important to ensure that team members don't abandon important individual values and ideas just to avoid conflict.

  - Leaders in this stage tend to operate more as facilitators than managers.

- **Performing**
  - The team possesses all the skills and knowledge needed.
  - Team members operate as a singular, holistic unit.
  - All team members are motivated to accomplish the team's goals.
  - When conflict arises, the team knows how to work through it.
  - Minimal supervision is needed.

Figure 3.1 provides a visual representation of the Tuckman model.

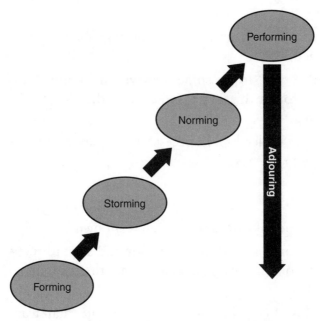

Figure 3.1 *Tuckman's Stages of Team Development*

When forming a new team for an agile project, it's natural to assume that armed with the right processes and tools, the team will jump to Norming or even Performing, but this is not usually the case. Strong leadership is needed to swiftly coach the team through the early stages of the team's maturity. This is why there is great value in keeping teams together that have worked well together in the past.

Resource
"Developmental sequence in small groups," Bruce Tuckman, *Psychological Bulletin* Volume 63, 1965.

Conflict

When teams work together to create or fix something, it's rare that everyone will agree on everything. Interacting and coming to consensus on project decisions can be fun for some and a real pain for others. Often teams don't always understand why some decisions are easier to make than others. Ralph Stacey described recommended strategies for group decision making based on agreement of the group and the level of uncertainty about the consequences of a decision (see Figure 3.2).

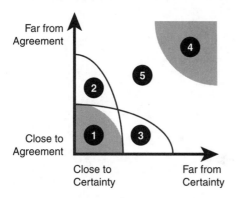

Figure 3.2 *Stacey's Zone of Complexity*

In Stacey's model, agreement refers to the degree to which members of the team concur about a proposed solution to a problem, design choice, importance of a task, or some other item that could potentially yield differing opinions. When the group is "close to agreement," most if not all members of the team are on the same page. When the group is "far from agreement," there could be multiple opinions, or there could be just a couple strong dissenting opinions.

Resource
Strategic Management and Organisational Dynamics, Second Edition, Ralph Stacey, Pitman, 1996.

Certainty refers to the access to information about past results based on similar decisions. If others made this same decision in the past, what were the results? What were the consequences? Although past results are no guarantee of future performance, they can be less risky than making decisions in a vacuum.

Based on the characteristics of each of Stacey's five zones, a team can employ strategies to optimize the decision-making process.

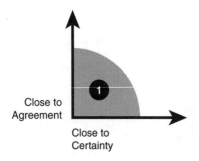

Figure 3.3 *Zone 1—high agreement, high certainty*

In zone 1 (see Figure 3.3), there is sufficient access to reliable data from the past related to the decision being made. Decision making is deterministic because a cause-and-effect relationship between a decision and its results/consequences can be drawn.

For example, if a team tries to determine how to design a user interface for a user to retrieve a forgotten password, numerous examples of previous designs for this problem exist. Each previous implementation has determinable characteristics related to security, user friendliness, and compatibility with the target implementation environment. The target solution can easily be designed based on other implementations that satisfy decision-making criteria specified by the team.

The safest strategy for this type of decision is to repeat what has been shown to work in the past. Tasks associated with these decisions tend to include research, data gathering—generally harvesting content and solutions that have worked in the past.

In this zone, there is virtually no negative impact to team dynamics, so no best practices are needed to maintain the unity of the team.

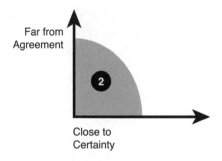

Figure 3.4 *Zone 2—low agreement, high certainty*

In zone 2 (see Figure 3.4), there is also sufficient historical information to offer predictability of future results.

However, there is still disagreement on the team. More often than not, disagreement has to do with different creative choices regarding aesthetics or usability.

The forgotten password example could fall into this zone if team members have different opinions about the look and feel of the user interface and/or the number of steps required to reset a password. Some solutions may be high in user friendliness but may expose security issues. In this example, team members may fall into different camps: Those championing user friendliness and those championing tight security.

In this zone, politics often come into play—idea selling, negotiation, and compromise. Critical thinkers on the team may develop matrices or decision trees to justify a choice. These could be met with resistance by those on the team who are not easily impressed with algorithms and models. It could also be met with resistance by other critical thinkers who would have chosen different decision-making criteria.

When decisions are made in this zone, shared team goals can be disrupted by these tactical choices. If a team had reached the performing stage, it could drift back a stage or two, although this is usually a temporary setback. When emotional moments caused by disagreement occur, it's important for team members to avoid taking criticism personally. This will be easier for some than others based on their behavioral profiles.

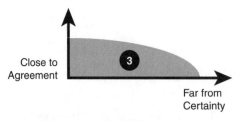

Figure 3.5 *Zone 3—high agreement, low certainty*

In zone 3 (see Figure 3.5), a cause-effect relationship between decisions and their consequences is indeterminable based on prior work. In this zone there may not be a rational explanation for general agreement on the team.

Resource
"Groupthink," William Whyte, Jr., *Fortune Magazine*, March 1952.

Although things may seem hunky-dory when in this zone, there is a danger in not paying attention to risks associated with uncertainty. It's not uncommon for a cohesive group in the performing stage to fall into the trap of groupthink. Groupthink happens when team members value a nonconfrontational work environment, and nobody on the team wants to do anything to stir things up.

In this zone, it's important to ensure that the team's consensus is not based on gut instinct or convenience. Instead, the team may need a reminder that decisions should be made based on the vision and goals of those funding the project. It may be useful to pay added attention to testing assumptions that are made and soliciting input from customers and others outside the team to reduce the risk of making poor decisions.

There's an inherent fallacy that to be a high-performing team, there should be little conflict. Actually, there can be great value in dissenting opinions if managed properly. See Chapter 5, "Collaboration," for more on how to capitalize on collaboration.

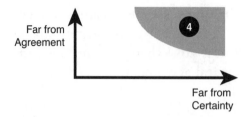

Figure 3.6 *Zone 4—zone of chaos: low agreement, low certainty*

When there is a high level of uncertainty about the outcome of a decision and a high degree of disagreement on the team, the environment can be chaotic and even hostile.

When a team enters zone 4, the zone of chaos (see Figure 3.6), there is a tendency to avoid decision making, especially by those who are averse to conflict. The churn caused by avoiding decisions of high importance can cause project delays and ultimately negatively affect the success of the project.

This zone tends to cultivate anarchy, so more rigid leadership may be needed to keep the team from regressing too far back into the "storming" stage. The team dynamics in this zone can be complex, and it's not realistic for management to prescribe a straightforward solution because a manager's guess about the appropriate course of action is as good (or as bad) as anyone else's.

A rational exit strategy from this zone is to either reduce uncertainty or increase agreement. Of the two factors, uncertainty may be the easiest variable to change. On a software project, uncertainty can be reduced with tactics such as prototyping, researching, and focus-group testing. Armed with more information, the team can drift back to zone 2 or zone 3 and employ the strategies for those zones.

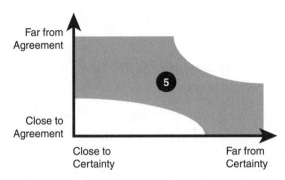

Figure 3.7 *Zone 5—the zone of complexity*

Not to be ignored, the area between the zone of chaos and the zones of rational, methodical decision making can be the most interesting (see Figure 3.7). When there are slight levels of agreement and the presence of some data to base decisions on, the team could drift toward zone 4 or back toward zones 1–3.

The environment in this zone tends to be entrepreneurial. This has the potential to cultivate creativity and the discovery of new ideas that could be innovative and profitable. This is the zone in which teams developing new products spend much of their time. This zone will be stimulating and enriching for some and exhausting and frustrating for others. The behavioral profile of team members can offer some predictability of how they will behave in the zone of complexity (see Chapter 2).

An example of a scenario that could occur in this zone is a team member who draws conclusions about the consequences of a decision based on collected data. Others on the team may question the validity of the data (and/or the assumptions that were made). When this happens, the scenario can play out differently based on the behavioral profile of the team members:

- A high D (dominator) may demand that others accept (or ignore) the data.

- A high I (influencer) may sell his/her opinion of the data.

- A high S (supporter) may feel uneasy with the disagreement that exists and try to encourage others to come to some level of agreement.

- A high C (critical thinker) may pour through Wikipedia, books, and documentation to find additional data to support the decision.

The primary goal of the team in this zone is to allow creativity and innovation to occur without drifting into the chaotic zone 4. Some may want to simplify the problem being solved so that a simpler decision-making processes in zones 1–3 could be employed. However, this could ignore complexity that can potentially lead to innovation and creativity and even in breakthrough results.

The identity and true mission of a project team will reveal itself in the zone of complexity, zone 5. If a team's primary motivator is to all get along while getting a project done, the net result may be tactical success (project is completed on time and under budget), yet they may not have experienced breakthrough results. This may be sufficient for some projects and insufficient for others.

Now What?

All these studies, theories, and stories might be interesting, but how can this information help your team?

When the topic of self-organizing arises, some people fear impending chaos, disorder, dysfunction, or worse. Putting it in civics terms, some think of anarchy. With no formal designated leadership, a team will eventually align or disband. When alignment happens, the direction it takes is completely directed by its membership. When self-organizing teams are employed on an agile project, it's imperative that the team includes representation of the goals of the business.

A key to getting value from the content of this book is to understand team dynamics and to learn how to adapt to the various situations a team finds itself in. It would be a fruitless endeavor to create a prescriptive decision-making model for teams. For example, not all decisions can be clearly articulated as a series of nonambiguous steps as could be depicted in a decision tree. Subjectivity is often present throughout projects, and subjectivity can trigger behavioral responses that must be dealt with.

Not all projects are created equal, and not all decisions made on a project are created equal. Team dynamics play a significant role in how a team handles unknowns and uncertainty, which are inevitable on most projects. Understanding those dynamics and why individuals behave the way they do in a situation can help a team focus and drive to resolution.

Human behavior is complex, and combining human beings to work together to solve problems and create things is exponentially more complex. There are numerous scientific studies and theories about individual behavior and team behavior that offer insight into the workings of a team. Access to the information in this chapter may offer some understanding of why teams behave the way they do and enable team members to behave with a more informed understanding of one another.

Closing

Armed with knowledge of the behavior of your team and why it behaves the way it does can be helpful to expose individual behaviors and team dynamics in a controlled setting. The Bridge exercise was designed to help a team capitalize on each other's strengths and optimize team dynamics in a high-pressure project situation.

Instructions for facilitating the Bridge Building exercise are found in Chapter 11, "Bridge Building."

Chapter 4

═══

Communication

After focusing on team dynamics, the team was behaving a little bit more like an agile team. They were self-managing and respectful of one another's behavioral styles. Lydia noticed, however, that some of the individuals were better at communicating than others. For example, she noticed that whenever a new idea was brought to Sean, he always initially responded with the words, "Yes, but..." This promoted a negative atmosphere. So Lydia decided to take a step back and discuss some general communication protocols with the team to foster a more productive environment.

Imagine a world without communication. On a typical day, consider how much communication is involved. In just the first few hours of a typical day, think about how many times you either send or receive some form of communication. Did you say "Good morning!" to the people you live with? Did you turn on the TV, open junk mail, read the newspaper, or send an email? We participate in most forms of communication without conscious awareness that we are communicating.

Figure 4.1 depicts Maslow's Hierarchy of Needs. According to Maslow, when core physiological needs in the base level are met (food, water, sleep, and so on), most of the remaining needs are fulfilled through some interaction with other people. In other words, communication is a seminal human need. Recall in the fictional movie *Castaway*, Tom Hank's character used a volleyball to create an artificial companion to fulfill his insatiable need to communicate.

Figure 4.1 *Maslow's Hierarchy of Needs*

Because communication is a core need of healthy people, you'd expect most people to work hard at becoming skillful communicators. In actuality, most people's communication skills could use significant improvement.

While reading this chapter, keep a conscious eye on your own communication skills and seek out areas for improvement. Adopting just a few of the tips here may help you significantly enhance the interactions you engage in on your project.

Lingo

When speaking or writing, you have many choices regarding language. Consider the following variations of the same statement:

- I want to talk to you about your business requirements.

- I need to talk to you about your business requirements.

- I'd like to talk to you about your business requirements.

- Let's talk about your business requirements.

- Let's talk about the business requirements.

- Can I talk to you about your business requirements?

- May I talk to you about your business requirements?

- We need to talk about your business requirements.

- You need to tell me about your business requirements.

Each of these nine statements seeks the same thing, but notice how each makes you feel as you read it. As you read them, imagine yourself as the speaker and then as the listener. Consider which of these puts you more at ease from both sides of the conversation.

As the old adage goes, "It's not necessarily what you say, but how you say it." Refined communication skills are the best tools you can have in your tool chest. There are many, many resources on effective communication skills. Most probably offer useful advice, and this book won't attempt to cover all the best practices of effective communication. Instead, we cover a collection of heavy hitters—those communication practices that tend to be redundantly emphasized in the pop psychology texts.

Whenever an adjective is clunked in front of the word communication, such as good, effective, high impact, and so on, the descriptor is always subjective. The polished presentation by the Cutko knife salesperson to a married couple may dazzle one member of the couple, yet annoy the other.

Therefore, when trying out the communication tips offered in this chapter, try experiencing them from both sides of the table. For example, as with the variations on a theme on the previous page, imagine yourself as the sender and as the receiver of each statement.

Empathy

In the spirit of seeing things from both sides, start with empathy. Empathy is identifying with another's perspective. Empathy is NOT, however, sympathy.

In the following scenario, Jane, an accountant, is discussing her job with Ron from the software development team:

> **Jane:** My job is stressful at the end of each month. I am required to put in a lot of overtime to close the books. My boss is high strung and is all over me to get my work done. It is annoying—I hate the last week of every month!

> **Sympathetic Ron:** I'm so sorry to hear that. I hate bosses like that—some bosses can be real jerks! What can I do to help reduce your workload and get your boss off your back?

> *versus*

> **Empathetic Ron:** I can imagine what it would be like to work under that type of pressure. A few years ago I had a job with similar circumstances, and I remember what it felt like.

Notice that sympathetic Ron is problem-solving Ron—the fixer. He is like the Mom kissing the child's boo-boo to make the pain go away.

Empathetic Ron is also understanding and may communicate that he "gets it." However, he may actually choose not to take sides. He expresses that he can see Jane's perspective but doesn't immediately pounce on the problem to fix it, sugar coat it, or pretend it isn't there.

On a project team, empathy can be a powerful tool. When empathy is genuine, a connection can exist between individuals that enhance their communication with each other. The wall that can exist between people often breaks away when an empathetic connection is made.

During requirements sessions on software projects, there is often an elephant in the room that nobody will discuss: We cannot build everything you have asked us to build. Some of the best-written user stories may never become software because they will be continuously overlooked during sprint planning meetings.

When a feature desired by one or a few is pushed down the priority list, emotions may enter the scene. At times like this, it's important not to back down and allow emotions to cause low-priority requirements to bloat the scope of a project. At the same time, understanding the perspective of the requirements' owner can help avoid the loss of commitment from those whose requirements were eliminated. An empathetic viewpoint can do two things:

- It can help validate that the decision to lower the priority of the feature was prudent.

- It can avoid sending mixed signals to those who are disappointed that they won't get their desired features.

Eye Contact

Many books have been written on body language, and in particular, eye contact. Generally in the Americas and in much of Europe, making eye contact with another indicates that you are listening and interested in what the other person has to say. When you look away, it implies that you are not paying attention, are uninterested, or disagree with what the other person has to say.

Your DISC tendencies may play a role in how you use eye contact. When a disagreeable comment is made to a D (dominator), the D may look at the speaker with a stern, forceful look. The look says, "I hear you, and I do not agree with what you are saying."

When a C (critical thinker) hears a disagreeable comment, the C may tend to look down or away from the speaker, hoping it will cause the speaker to stop talking.

In the same scenario with an S (supporter), the S is likely to make eye contact with raised eyebrows, exposing negative feelings regarding the comment.

Although those who have a high degree of I (influencer) tend to use eye contact a lot, when listening to another person speak, the I is most likely thinking, "Why is this person speaking? I want to be speaking. How can I capture control of this conversation?"

A lot can be stated nonverbally through effective use of eye contact. A person who maintains eye contact can maintain control of an interaction, especially when the other person looks away.

Overuse or abuse of eye contact could make others uncomfortable, especially if there are possible relationship implications. In some Muslim cultures, for example, eye contact between males and females is frowned upon. In any culture, there is a tipping point between a gaze that indicates sincere interest and a gaze that indicates, "I'm feigning interest." Eye contact when combined with variations of other facial expressions—raised eyebrows, smile/frown, and so on can take on completely different meanings.

Ambiguity

Ambiguous communication tends to waste enormous amounts of time on a project. When information is expressed accurately, clearly, and without a trace of ambiguity, individuals are best served to interact and solve a problem or make a decision.

When ambiguity is introduced, however, misinterpretations and assumptions are often made, which slow down the productivity of the interaction.

A group of individuals in a meeting room were presented with the following instructions: "Draw a pizza that has eight slices with three lines." Pen and paper in hand, many of the participants looked puzzled. A couple of folks with inquisitive expressions raised their hands, which caused the facilitator to say, "Let's see who can solve the puzzle the fastest; then I'll address your questions."

This simple puzzle becomes impossible to many who try to solve it because they impose constraints that just aren't there.

Many will complain that the possible solutions depicted in Figure 4.2 violate the instructions:

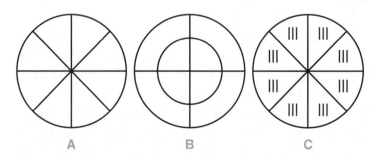

Figure 4.2 *Pizza Puzzle solutions*

Solution A may be disputed by those who imposed an unstated constraint that the pizza can only have three lines. Solution B may be disputed by those required themselves to use only straight lines. In Solution C, each slice has three lines. Most listeners probably inferred that the pizza must have three lines, but the statement could be interpreted as each slice has three lines.

The point of this tricky little exercise isn't about fooling people; it's about how even the most straightforward sounding instruction could be interpreted differently by members of a group. When people assume the message was clear, and they impose their own constraints, waste and mistakes can happen.

Body Language

A lot has also been written about body language. Without saying a word, your stance alone can speak volumes. Often, it's likely that you are not thinking about or feeling what your body is saying that causes others to misread you.

In Shakespeare's *Othello*, Othello sensed an uneasiness in the demeanor of his wife Desdemona, which he interpreted as evidence that she had been unfaithful to him. In actuality, Desdemona had been faithful to Othello, and her uneasiness was due to fear that Othello wouldn't believe her. Othello's misinterpretation of Desdemona's nonverbal cues lead to his murdering her.

There is a lot of popular interest in interpretation of nonverbal communication. Television shows such as "Lie to Me" and "Psych" depict characters with acute awareness of nonverbal clues that most people overlook.

Dr. Maureen Sullivan from the University of San Francisco tested 13,000 individuals to assess their ability to detect deception by others. Of the 13,000 people, only 31 could consistently detect deception by others.

Although accurate reading of nonverbal clues is not something everyone can do, most people do tend to interpret nonverbal communication by others, whether it is an accurate interpretation or not. This leads to perceptions that could be wrong.

The focus of this section of the book is therefore not about how to interpret others' nonverbal cues. Rather, it is how to better manage your own body language to avoid misinterpretation by others. This is called body language self-awareness.

The definitive body language signal is folded arms (as shown in Figure 4.3). When talking to someone whose arms are folded, the popular interpretation is that the arm folder is rejecting or disagreeing with what is being said. In reality, the person could be cold. Perhaps the person is more comfortable with folded arms. It's not necessarily an indicator of rejection. Unfortunately, actual intent is irrelevant.

Figure 4.3 *Body language self-awareness*

When Fred is talking to Mary, and Mary's arms are folded, it's possible (and even highly probable) that Fred will interpret Mary's folded arms as rejection of his ideas. The typical observer will look at this situation from Fred's point of view: "What is Mary telling me?" Let's try looking at it from the other direction—Mary's point of view: "Fred is talking to me. I want to fold my arms, but if I do, Fred may think I'm disagreeing with him. It would really be so much more comfortable to fold my arms, but I'm just not going to."

Mary's self-awareness of her body language demonstrated empathy toward Fred. Whether or not Mary agreed with what Fred was saying, her conscientious decision to avoid telegraphing negativity offered Fred more freedom to express his thoughts.

The key message here is not that Mary has to agree with Fred. Rather, Mary is empathetic to Fred's desire to express his ideas freely. The empathetic Mary is more likeable than the (presumed) rejecting Mary, which offers an opportunity for Mary and Fred to have a richer, more engaging interaction on the subject they're discussing.

Your nonverbal cues may be unconsciously sending a message to others. The characters in Figure 4.4 show an exaggerated expression of nonverbal "shouting." Without uttering a word, these characters (from left to right) clearly depict arrogance, confidence, and disapproval. See Figure 4.5 for common interpretations of body language.

Figure 4.4 *Nonverbal cues*

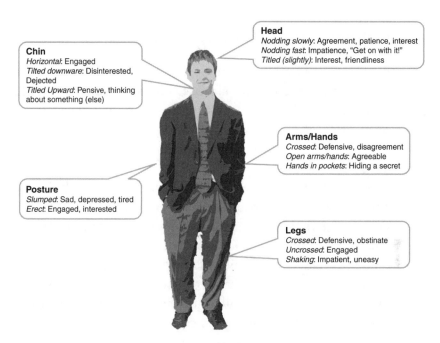

Head
Nodding slowly: Agreement, patience, interest
Nodding fast: Impatience, "Get on with it!"
Titled (slightly): Interest, friendliness

Chin
Horizontal: Engaged
Tilted downware: Disinterested, Dejected
Titled Upward: Pensive, thinking about something (else)

Arms/Hands
Crossed: Defensive, disagreement
Open arms/hands: Agreeable
Hands in pockets: Hiding a secret

Posture
Slumped: Sad, depressed, tired
Erect: Engaged, interested

Legs
Crossed: Defensive, obstinate
Uncrossed: Engaged
Shaking: Impatient, uneasy

Figure 4.5 *Common interpretations of body language*

Cultural Awareness

Nonverbal communication is not necessarily a universal language. The thumbs-up gesture is often used in the United States to indicate agreement and affirmation. The same gesture in Italy means the number one, yet in American Sign Language it means the number 10; and thumbs up in many Middle Eastern countries is considered an obscene, insulting gesture.

Thumbs up is a fairly overt gesture. More subtle is a gentle rocking of the head from side to side, which in many cultures means disagreement. However, the side-to-side gesture in India is seen as a sign of agreement. Misinterpreting this nonverbal cue can often confuse westerners visiting India.

Reflecting Body Language

Echoing the body language of a person you interact with can be interpreted as empathetic. For example, if you talk to someone who leans forward with uncrossed legs and open arms, if you reflect the same pose, you are sending the message: "I am engaged in this interaction, and you have my attention."

Be prudent when reflecting, though. It could backfire and be interpreted as mocking. It's also not helpful to reflect a pose that has negative elements. For example, when talking to someone who leans back with arms crossed behind the head, it would be counterproductive to reflect the same negative pose. Instead, you might succeed in drawing the other person more fully into the conversation by leaning forward and engaging eye contact.

Small Talk

Conversations often stray from project-related topics. This is inevitable with even the most focused, driven members of a project team. Discussing the weather, yesterday's football game, or the price of tea in China may seem to be a waste of time at work. However, this "small talk" can contribute to the communication dynamics of members of the project team.

In the 2009 movie "The Invention of Lying," characters live in a world in which all thoughts are freely expressed with complete openness and honesty. Nobody tells lies, and nobody withholds information. This leads to unexpected conversations with everyone blurting out what they actually think. These conversations are unlikely in real life, not because all people are liars, but rather because most people tend to withhold thoughts or disguise sensitive and personal interactions with those that are nondescript. This "language" of topics that are mundane and noncontroversial is referred to as small talk.

Most people have a love/hate relationship with small talk. Consider the following interaction. Dave Developer is reluctantly attending the mandatory project kick-off event in the company cafeteria. All members of the project team will be there, along with business executives who will be funding the project (and beneficiaries of the software created by the project).

Barbara Business-Stakeholder had been looking forward to the get-together all week. She was excited about meeting and chatting with all members of the project team. Barbara enjoys things like this—Barbara's favorite part of her job is talking with people.

Dave, on the other hand, was stressed about the whole thing. What was the point of the social event anyway? A bunch of people standing around jibber-jabbering about meaningless dribble. Dave would go because it was expected, but he was not happy about wasting time talking about things that will not advance the progress of the project.

Table 4.1 presents a snippet of a conversation between Dave and Barbara as they meet. The first column indicates what was said (the small talk), and the second column shows what the speaker actually meant (a literal translation of the small talk).

Table 4.1 *What Was Said and What Was Meant*

	What Was Said	What Was Meant
Barbara	Hello Dave.	His nametag says "Dave." I don't know him, and he's not talking to anyone, so I'll go ahead and break the ice.
Dave	Hi Barbara.	Okay, here it comes...
Barbara	What is your role on the project?	So let's see if we have anything to talk about.
Dave	I'm a software developer.	Asked and answered.
Barbara	Sure has been hot outside this week!	I know nothing about software development, so let's shift to something I do know about. I'll pick something safe... noncontroversial...something that he's certain to respond to. After all, there's nothing worse than hitting a dead end in a conversation.
Dave	Yup, sure has been hot.	What a lame topic. There's nothing more boring than talking about the weather. See, I knew this thing was going to be a waste of my time.
Barbara	Are you excited about the project?	Okay, he hasn't abandoned the conversation, so let's dive into something more relevant.
Dave	I don't know that much about the project yet. What do you know about it?	Hmmm...maybe this lady does have something real to talk about.
Barbara	Well, I am head of one of the departments that will be the primary users of the new system. We are excited about getting this new system built.	You may not be interested in talking to me, but I want you to know that I am someone important who you will want to get along with.
Dave	Oh, I look forward to getting to know more about what your expectations are for the new system.	This is someone who will likely determine the success or failure of the work we do, so I'll want to get along with her!

Clearly, what had started as a dry small talk session turned into an important meeting for both Dave and Barbara. Agile projects can succeed or fail based on the quality of the communication on the team.

For communication to occur between individuals, some form of a relationship must be formed. If Barbara were to discuss the weather with Frank, the cashier at the grocery store, that relationship may be fleeting. Barbara might have never met Frank before, and she may never see him again. The small talk she strikes up with Frank has no long-term purpose. She is just being friendly in this case.

The small talk that Barbara uses to launch a conversation with Dave Developer, on the other hand, has a more lasting purpose. She is breaking the ice with someone with whom she'll be working on an important project. It would seem odd to dive directly into rich, intense subject matter. The small talk serves as a warm up that allows a productive working relationship to begin to form.

Collaborative Conversations

If a tree falls in a forest does it make a sound? If something is communicated and nobody hears it or reads it, was it actually communicated? Philosophy aside, from this point forward, assume that at least two parties are required for any form of communication to exist.

The next chapter delves more deeply into collaboration. For now, however, the focus is on collaboration that occurs during a conversation. In oral communication, when speakers and listeners come together, there are increasingly rich levels of collaboration.

When speakers and listeners are brought together, there must be a match between speaking strategy and listening strategy for a productive interaction to occur. When a mismatch occurs between the level of collaboration desired by speaker and listeners, speakers and listeners tend to get frustrated.

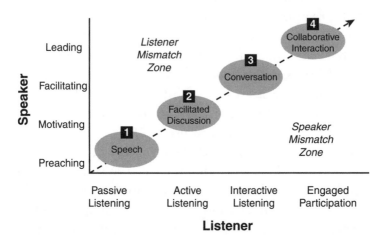

Figure 4.6 *Collaborative communication levels*

In any given combination of speaker/listeners, the maturity of collaborative communication often aligns with one of the four levels depicted in Figure 4.6:

- **Level 1: Speech:** A speaker is preaching and/or motivating the listeners, who are often a mixture of passive and active listeners.

- **Level 2: Facilitated Discussion:** The speaker takes on more of a facilitation role, engaging listeners to contribute to the topic being discussed.

- **Level 3: Conversation:** At this level, the speaker and listeners engage in a dialogue, where speaker/listener roles are swapped continuously. The originating speaker role may set the tone and direction, after which others involved in the conversation steer its direction.

- **Level 4: Collaborative Interaction:** At level 4, complete collaboration occurs between members of the group. The speaker/listener roles swap out frequently and swiftly. Members of the group work together toward a common goal (solving a problem, discussing an issue, resolving a need, and so on). At this level, the group takes on its own identity.

Collaborative interaction is a desirable place for a project team to get to and remain at. When a project team reaches this level, members tend to work together to fulfill each other's communication needs. At this level, communication is leveraged as a tool to advance the progress of a project. When a communication block is reached, other members of the team may step in to ensure that progress is continued.

In improvisational theater, a group of performers work together to create a cohesive (and usually humorous) entertainment piece without a script. Television shows such as *Whose Line Is It Anyway?* and *Curb Your Enthusiasm* have showcased improvisational performers. On *Curb Your Enthusiasm*, a rough sketch of a story idea is presented to the actors, who create the story together in front of rolling cameras rather than reading lines from a script. The pressure of this real-time collaboration draws the best possible work out of each contributor. On *Whose Line Is It Anyway?* the performers have the added pressure of creating entertaining content in front of a live audience.

One of the greatest challenges of "improv" (as this is commonly called), is the live collaboration that occurs between multiple performers. All members of an improv team know how to capitalize on each other's strengths and overcome each other's weaknesses. A goal of an improv troupe is to keep communication flowing with no dead air.

Popular "improv" practices can help foster better communication on teams, such as the following:

- **Keep it flowing:** Improv masters are skillful at keeping communication flowing, and team members all work together to make the "scene" a success. If one person dominates at the expense of others, the group fails. If one person falters, others will jump in to keep things going.

- **Say "Yes, and...":** By responding to a teammate's contribution with "Yes, and..." you are make a commitment to adding to what has already been offered. This approach maintains cohesion by committing to build upon what was started. It also shifts the burden of enhancing the overall contribution.

  Mary   I believe customers will want a user interface that is attractive and is easy to use.

  Fred   Yes, and...

  After the "and," Fred adds new information. The person who says, "Yes, and..." is expected to contribute new content, not just restate or transform what was already said.

  Fred   Yes, and the screen should be clean with few widgets, options, and displayed content.

  Jane   Yes, and the system should be fast, too. New windows should pop up within just a second or two from the time they are requested.

  David   Yes, and... [Continues until the group runs out of steam.]

- **Avoid blocking:** Blocking is the opposite of "Yes, and..." Expressing a negative reaction to the previous contribution can stop the conversation flow dead in its tracks. It may be simply saying, "No," or it could be ignoring the conversation and shifting to a completely different subject. A high D (dominator) is likely to block when in disagreement with an idea that is being cultivated.

Mary   I believe customers will want a user interface that is attractive and easy to use.

Pat   No, actually customers will want a feature-rich application with a lot of information and user-configurable capabilities.

OR

Pat   I'm not that concerned about the user interface; it's the speed of the application that I'm worried about.

- **Avoid questions:** Asking questions could be perceived as a "punt," which shifts the burden to someone else. This is a common tactic of a high C (critical thinker), who may believe that critical questions are contributing to the team. Rather, they demonstrate that the questioner doesn't want to play the game and is quick to shift the "hot potato" to someone else.

Mary   I believe customers will want a user interface that is attractive and is easy to use.

Derek   Are you familiar with the corporate user interface style guide and the standard UI templates?

OR

Derek   How do you define "easy to use?"

Notice how Derek's questions push the burden immediately back to Mary. This places responsibility on Mary to keep the conversation flowing, and Derek plays a minor role in the overall results of the group, even though Derek probably feels that his inquisitive style is helping.

- **Include other team members:** Help draw in other team members who are not contributing by providing information they can build on. This requires an awareness of skills and interests of those team members. Notice the collaborative helpful tone of Mary and David's exchange:

> Mary   I believe customers will want a user interface that is attractive and is easy to use. David, I remember that the user interfaces you developed on other projects were well accepted by your users. How can we achieve the same success on this project?

> David   Well, I should conduct a focus group with key target users. Also Derek is a pro at screen layouts. We'll want to get him involved.

- **Be Socratic:** The great teacher and philosopher Socrates devised a teaching technique that broke from the conventions of his time. Rather than blurt knowledge, he posed a series of questions to his students. This allowed the students to navigate their own path of understanding and learning. These questions allow a speaker to clarify and qualify what is being said.

Warning
There's a fine line between being a Socratic questioner and being annoying.

Note that asking questions is a "no no" in the improv world because it is seen as deflecting involvement. A Socratic series of questions, however, encourages active involvement by the questioner. As a facilitation technique, it can keep people on task and help them avoid getting off track from the goals of the communication session. With this technique, the facilitator is not questioning what is being said. Rather, the facilitator is asking questions to encourage the speaker to elaborate, enhance, and clarify what is being said.

Examples of helpful Socratic questions:

- *What makes you say that?*
- *Can you describe an example of what you're talking about?*
- *How does this align with what others have been saying?*
- *How does this differ from what others have been saying?*
- *Are there other ways to ask what you are asking?*

And a few metaquestions (questions about the question itself):

- *Did the way you worded the question get the response you expected?*
- *Is that a good question to be asking?*
- *Why is what you are saying important to the project?*

- **Be even more Socratic:** Another technique often attributed to Socrates is to feign ignorance—to pretend to have no knowledge of something you are fully knowledgeable about. Listen in on the following conversation:

Fred	Would you like me to explain the steps involved in underwriting an insurance policy?
Jane	[Having spent the past 20 years as an insurance underwriter and holding various certifications as a certified underwriter, bites her tongue, feigns curiosity and interest, and says...] Yes, please tell us about it.

Feigning ignorance can be difficult for those who are knowledgeable on a subject. Their egos entice them to let everyone know how smart they are. By swallowing pride and feigning ignorance, though, there is a great opportunity to augment their knowledge with another's perspective.

In the preceding scenario, if Jane had not allowed Fred to continue, she might have lost the opportunity to either validate what she knows or add to her knowledge of the subject.

The Power of Shutting Up

When used properly, silence can be a powerful communication tool. Proper use of silence includes appropriate choice of supporting eye contact and other body language.

In this scenario, Fred is undecided about whether to include a certain feature in the scope of the system. Jane (who is likely a high D and/or a high I) feels that it's necessary to say something:

Fred	I can't quite decide whether that feature is important and should be included in the scope of the system.
Jane	I think it's quite important. I'd include it if I were you.

OR

Okay, what can I do to help you decide?

OR

When will you decide?

If instead Jane had said nothing, she could have urged Fred to come to a decision. If Jane looked Fred in the eyes and leaned forward, she would silently be saying, "Take your time, Fred, I'll wait for you to think about it and come to a decision."

If Fred happens to be a high C, he is unlikely to make a snap decision and will want time to think about the implications of his decision before announcing it. By exercising restraint and using silence with appropriate body language, Jane allowed Fred to make a more informed, well-thought-out decision.

Using silence as a tool can be difficult for high D's and high I's. Silence can drive these people nutty, and they'll likely try to fill it with sound.

Communication Latency

In 1860, a message crossed the United States from coast to coast in ten days via Pony Express. Today, it's possible for an email message to make the same journey in less than a second.

This doesn't mean, however, that email is the definitive communication speed test benchmark. Email has its place but does not guarantee efficiency or speed. You probably have messages in your email inbox from more than ten days ago that were overlooked or not read. If, however, someone rode up alongside you on a horse and handed you a letter that had been in transit for the past ten days, there's a good chance that you'd drop whatever you're doing to read it.

Communication latency refers to the delay that occurs from the time something is communicated until the time it is received and processed. A common goal of an agile project is to reduce communication latency. Real-time interactions can keep a project moving forward, whereas delays can have a compounding detrimental impact to the project. Figure 4.7 depicts commonly used communication tactics, shown with increasing amounts of latency (or delay) from when the sender sends the message and the recipient receives the message.

As an example, receiving the message does not mean that it arrived in the recipient's inbox. The communication transaction is complete when the recipient reads and understands what was communicated. It's ironic that some of the more popular modern tactics actually introduce the most latency.

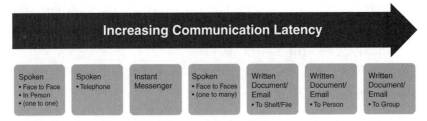

Figure 4.7 *Increasing communication latency*

The more time that passes from the sending of information and the processing of that information, the greater the risk the information will be misunderstood, ignored, or misused. Notably, the context that was in existence at the time something is communicated will likely have changed as more time passes. This causes information to be processed out of context, which can lead to misinterpretation.

Ideally, all project communication would occur live and in real time. Behaviorally, real-time conversations are fun and desirable for a high I (influencer); at the same time they can be exhausting and undesirable to a high C (critical thinker). When Mary asks Derek to do some research on a certain business requirement and to let her know what he finds out, his follow-up actions will depend on his behavioral tendencies.

Because Derek is a high DI, he may likely do a cursory job of researching (or try to delegate it) and will report what he learns back to Mary in person. Derek is likely to report back to Mary within hours so he can get the to-do item off his list.

When Derek tells Mary what he has learned, he will consider his task complete. If Mary were to ask Derek to write up what he discussed, Derek is likely to be frustrated or annoyed.

If Mary had asked Carl instead, she would have experienced a different response because Carl is a high C. Carl is likely to take his time doing a thorough job of researching the problem. When he has researched to his satisfaction, he will likely write up the information and send it to Mary in an email message. It's highly unlikely that Carl will call Mary or see her in person to discuss what he learned. After Carl clicked "send" he considered his task complete. If the email server crashed and the message never made it to Mary, Carl would likely have never pursued making sure Mary received and understood the information.

The contrast between Derek's and Carl's behavior is important. Carl probably did a much more thorough and accurate job of addressing Mary's needs. However, the delay in getting the information to Mary could have potentially caused other delays. Additionally, if Mary never received (or noticed) the reply, Carl's work was pointless.

On the other hand, Derek handled the request in a timely manner, but the quality of his research was probably much poorer than what Carl produced.

In either case, it's productive for all team members to maintain awareness of communication latency and to work to minimize delays in communication threads.

We the People...

Here's a quick grammar lesson:

- First-person singular: "I..."

- Second-person singular: "You..." Third-person singular: "He/she..."

- First-person plural: "We..." Second-person plural: "You..."

- Third-person plural: "They..."

Regardless of your intent, when you choose to speak in first-person versus third-person, and singular versus plural, others' perception of you will likely be affected by what they hear. Generally:

- Those who use first-person singular can be perceived as arrogant and boring. Others' eyes may glaze over as you continually say, "I this," and "I that." That doesn't mean you mustn't ever talk about yourself. However, it's a good idea to monitor your "me" speak and be cognoscente of a lack of empathy for your listeners.

- Those who use second-person can be perceived as nagging or preaching. Listeners tend to get defensive and raise their guard when they hear, "You this," and "You that." The "You" speaker may also be seen as arrogant, which is often a turn off to listeners.

- Those who frequently speak in the third-person may be viewed as gossips. When you choose to talk about others, be aware that any hint of judgment or criticism could cause you to be labeled as a critic and a gossip. People may be less inclined to be open with you to avoid being judged or criticized by you.

- The use of first-person plural is a great way to get collective buy-in for whatever you have to say. When you say "we," others see you as part of the team, a member of the family, someone who has the same skin in the game that they do. Not only can this tactic help you avoid alienation, it can encourage others to be more open with you.

Closing

The following tables summarize key contents of this chapter from the DISC behavioral perspective:

Table 4.2 *A High D (Dominator) Likely Exhibits These Tendencies*

Behavior Area	Tendency
Eye contact	Looks you straight in the eye.
Body language	Exhibits confidence. Walks quickly. Speaks loudly. May look at watch frequently.
Collaborative conversations	May monopolize conversations. May not allow others who are not high D's to easily contribute their own ideas.
Socratic questioning	May not question because they assume their own views and ideas are the correct ones.
Feigning ignorance	Likely not to feign ignorance because that may show lack of confidence.
Grammar: First versus second versus third	Likely to use first-person more than most. It is about me. Will also use second-person to get someone to do something.

Table 4.3   *A High I(Influencer) Likely Exhibits These Tendencies*

Behavior Area	Tendency
Body language	Very expressive. Wears their emotions on their sleeves.
Collaborative conversations	May monopolize conversation but will want to hear what others have to say. May stray off topic.
Socratic questioning	Will be the most likely to do this. Will want to draw out what others have to say.
Feigning ignorance	Although confident, will do this if it is a way to get others to speak up.
Grammar: first versus second versus third	Likely to use first-person plural and third-person plural the most. It is about the team, and gossip is OK.

Table 4.4   *A High S (Supporter) Likely Exhibits These Tendencies*

Behavior area	Tendency
Eye contact	May not make good eye contact.
Body language	Reserved.
Collaborative conversations	Will contribute and want to make sure that everyone on the team gets to contribute. If too many D's or I's are in the discussion, may not get a word in edgewise.
Socratic questioning	Will want to do this. Will care what others feel or believe.
Feigning ignorance	Will be the most likely to do this to get others to share their feelings and ideas.
Grammar: first versus second versus third	Likely to use first-person plural the most. It is all about the team.

Table 4.5 *A High C (Critical Thinker) Likely Exhibits These Tendencies*

Behavior area	Tendency
Eye contact	Often looks away.
Body language	Reserved. Chin down. Methodical.
Collaborative conversations	Will contribute after they hear the facts and/or when asked for an opinion. If too many D's or I's in the discussion, may not speak up even if they have the best solution.
Socratic questioning	May do this in search of the correct resolution.
Feigning ignorance	Will likely not do this.
Grammar: first versus second versus third	Likely to use first-person or third-person plural the most.

Chapter 5

Collaboration

Now that the team members were all communicating effectively, it was time to start garnering the strength of the team as a whole. Each individual on the team was extremely bright, but Lydia knew that if the team understood and applied the "Wisdom of Crowds," it would make the team even more effective.

Moreover, Lydia witnessed some of the natural conflicts that often arise between traditional roles on software project teams. For example, there seemed to be a constant tension between Lisa (who was a tester) and Eric (a developer). This is what Lydia referred to as the yin-yang on software projects. This is one of the reasons why agile teams contain fewer separations of roles and all team members are expected to do whatever is necessary (within their capabilities) for the team to succeed.

Working as a Team

Recall back in school when the teacher announced the requirements for a project, including that the assignment is to be completed in teams of four. Although an occasional student may cherish the opportunity to share the workload, many may likely dread the hassles of working as a group.

Attitudes about collaboration tend to align closely with DISC tendencies. A high D (dominator) doesn't mind collaborating, as long as everyone else agrees with what he says. A high I (influencer) enjoys the social aspects of collaboration—a captive audience. A high S (supporter) is okay with collaboration as long as everyone is getting along okay, and a high C (critical thinker) tends to see collaboration as interference with getting work done.

Teamwork tends to be work in and of itself. Coordinating times to meet, determining who is best qualified to complete each of the tasks, and ensuring that everyone is contributing their fair share of the workload—these are all givens when working as a team. The most annoying component of teamwork, though, is that others may disagree with you.

Debates, arguments, selling ideas, these are the stuff of teamwork. They can be arduous, time-consuming, and the source of tremendous frustration. Given all these "costs" of teamwork, is it worth it?

Vox Populi

In an article published in the prestigious scientific journal *Nature* in March 1907, statistician Francis Galton reported the results of a study he performed on data collected at a stock and poultry exhibition in Plymouth, England. Galton titled the article, "Vox Populi," a Latin expression that means "the voice of the people," or the opinion of the general public.

As the 800 ticket holders entered the exhibition, they were offered the opportunity to guess the weight of an ox after it had been slaughtered and dressed. A prize was offered to the person with the closest estimate, so ticket holders put some diligence in their guessing. All ticket holders wrote their estimates on the backs of their entry tickets, along with their names and addresses so that they could be contacted if they won.

The stock and poultry exhibition attracted a variety of visitors. Some were butchers or farmers, who may have had expertise in estimating the weight of cattle, whereas others might not have known the difference between an ox and a cow. A scientific approach to ascertaining the weight of the ox based on the estimates might have placed more weight (no pun intended) on the expert's estimates. However, Galton had a hypothesis that in a heterogeneous group of people, the best estimate would be found smack dab in the middle.

In a previous article titled "One Vote, One Value," Galton contended that in any group that must ascertain an ordinal value, each participant should be given one vote and that all votes carry equal weight. The optimal number can then be found in the middle. Galton contended that the middle is key—the median, not the mean, should be used. This prevents what he referred to as "cranks" from overly influencing the results.

Resources

"One Vote, One Value," Francis Galton, *Nature* 75, 1907.

As an illustration, when a jury awards a financial settlement, using the mean (or straight average) can lead to skewed results. In a civil case in which the jury determines how much to award the plaintiff, it's possible for the settlement amount to be heavily biased by a single juror. For example, consider the following civil case in which a six-person jury is charged with determining the amount to be awarded:

Juror 1	$100,000
Juror 2	$ 90,000
Juror 3	$ 80,000

Juror 4	$110,000
Juror 5	$120,000
Juror 6	$ 85,000

Using a straight average, the award amount is $97,500. Using the median, the award amount is $95,000. Often, the mean and median are close.

However, if Juror 1 chose to influence the award amount upward by choosing a settlement amount of two million dollars, the average jumps to approximately $414,000. The median value, however, would rise slightly to $100,000. Therefore, use of median offers a less-biased representation of the desires of the group.

So back to the livestock exhibition: The exhibitioners loaned the box of entry tickets to Galton, who analyzed the estimates of the weight of the ox. After discarding 13 illegible entries, Galton calculated the median as 1,207 pounds, which was within 0.8% of the actual weight of 1,198 pounds. In plotting the estimates, there was no symmetry—the estimates ranged widely. However, the middle proved to be extremely close to the correct value.

Jack Treynor wrote an article in the *Financial Analysts Journal* about a jellybean experiment he conducted with students in a Finance class he was teaching at the University of Southern California.

Resources
"Market Efficiency and the Bean Jar Experiment," Jack Treynor, *Financial Analysts Journal* 43, 1987.

Professor Treynor put jellybeans in a jar and had 56 students guess how many there were. The average of the group was 871, which was closer to the actual number (850) than all but one of the students.

Resources

The Wisdom of Crowds, Why the Many Are Smarter than the Few and How Collective Wisdom Shapes Business, Economies, Societies, and Nations, James Surowiecki, 2004.

James Surowiecki discusses this concept in his popular book *The Wisdom of Crowds*, and he has conducted the jelly-bean counting experiment with his audiences during speaking engagements. The average of all the guesses in the room is usually within 3% to 5% of the actual number of jellybeans, and the average is usually closer to the actual number than more than 95% of the guesses.

Although Treynor and Surowiecki chose to use mean (average) instead of median, as Galton had done, the sample size was most likely large enough to dilute the impact of bias imposed by a few participants.

Sean, a colleague at Improving Enterprises, tried this out at a wedding he attended. As individuals signed the guestbook when they got to the reception, they were asked to jot down a guess for the number of jellybeans in a jar. Sean glanced down the list of guesses that had been written down so far, calculated a quick average, and submitted that as his guess. Sean's guess was closest to the mark, and he won a prize—the jar of jellybeans!

Group Survival

Years ago, the U.S. and U.K. militaries developed team building exercises that helped participants understand the *power of many*. The *power of many* is a label used to describe how a group in and of itself has greater wisdom than that of any individual within that group. NASA later developed its own version for training astronauts, and it now offers this exercise for the general public's use.

Instructions and materials for the NASA Moon Survival exercise can be found in Chapter 12, "Moon Survival." Everything needed to conduct this exercise with a group is included. It's suggested that the facilitator read through all the material to become familiar with it, and that the participants not read about it so that they can participate more fully in the exercise.

Moon Survival and other similar exercises provide participants with experiential understanding of the benefits of group interaction. This is particularly useful with high C team members, who often get frustrated by the effort required and time spent when participating in group interactions.

Problem-Solving Versus Decision Making

In a typical project setting, many decisions are made. Individuals make some decisions, whereas other decisions are made by groups of people. There are not necessarily any official definitions for the terms decision making and problem solving, so any interpretation is valid. For the purposes of this book, the following distinction will be used:

- **Problem solving:** A series of tasks focused on determining, testing, and implementing solutions to a given problem.

- **Decision making:** The process of making a choice for each step of a problem-solving process.

Hence, problem solving can involve a lot of decision making, and the purpose of most decisions is usually to support a larger problem-solving effort.

The value in distinguishing between problem solving and decision making is to better understand the motivations and dynamics of each.

Individuals and Decisions

The DISC tendencies of an individual can influence how decisions are made and how problems are solved. Bearing in mind that problem solving is heavily dependent on decision making, the efficiency and quality of decision making can influence the productivity of an individual.

A team member who is a high D will usually make decisions with little hesitation and often with little interaction. A team member who is a high I is comfortable making decisions quickly and without proof of all the facts. He will tend to trust team member's opinions and will take an optimistic point of view. A team member who is a high S is likely to make slower decisions and will want to hear all the inputs of the team. A team member who is a high C will usually not feel comfortable making a decision unless she knows all the facts and has time to analyze and contemplate them.

Groups and Decisions

In addition to individual behavioral tendencies, it's also important to recognize that the DISC makeup of a group of people can greatly influence the approach the group will use to make decisions. It can also affect the quality of decisions; therefore, it's helpful to recognize how a team's DISC mix is affecting its decision-making behavior.

A DISC-homogeneous group is one that is made up of individuals with predominant membership from one of the four DISC profiles. Recall that most everyone has some D, I, S, and C but that usually one or two of these are the dominant in an individual's behavioral tendencies.

DISC-homogeneous groups are not unusual, especially on teams made up of people with similar backgrounds, skills, and roles. A team of computer programmers could have a predominance of high C members, whereas a team of marketing people may be made up of mostly high I members. In a congressional committee meeting, it's likely that most members of the committee are high D's.

Group Influence

A typical individual within a given group often conforms to the will of the group. In the jellybean exercise described earlier in this chapter, the guesses were blind; each guesser does not have access to the rest of the group's guesses (with the exception of Sean at the wedding reception.)

Because free will is always at play, not all groups will necessarily demonstrate conformance behavior. It's useful to have awareness of the behavioral tendencies of a team you are working on. It is often worth investing some time assessing whether a team demonstrates more conformant behavior or more discordant behavior. Conformant versus discordant isn't an either/or condition. Teams tend to have varying degrees of conformity. The graph in Figure 5.1 is a conceptual depiction of this scale. In decision-making situations, teams that center on one or just a couple closely related decision points is considered highly conformant. On the other end of the scale are teams with widely varying opinions. These teams are considered highly discordant.

On highly discordant teams, making a decision isn't likely as simple as finding the median point among the opinions of all team members. This isn't usually practical, and for subjective decisions that have no concretely measurable value, this isn't even possible. Awareness of the team's adaptability to the wisdom of the overall group can help leaders be more productive when facilitating group decisions.

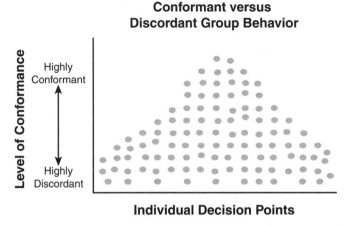

Figure 5.1 *Assessing the group influence of a team*

As a ScrumMaster assigned to a new team, John wanted to determine how conformant or discordant the team was going to be. John got the team together and asked them to each guess how much he weighed, writing down their guesses on a piece of paper.

John gathered up the guesses without making any note of who made which guess and plotted them on a chart. John noticed that the estimates ranged from 155 pounds to 220 pounds, with various guesses at points in between those numbers.

Next, John showed the chart to everyone on the team and asked each person to review the chart and make another private guess at his weight. Again, John gathered up the guesses, plotted them, and showed the plotted data to everyone. After one more round of guesses, John made a final plot (see Figure 5.2).

After three rounds, John learned a few things about the team. Notice how the data clusters closer together during the second round and even closer during the third round. This is an indicator to John that the team exhibits conformant behavior. This helps raise John's awareness of how the team is likely to behave in collaborative situations.

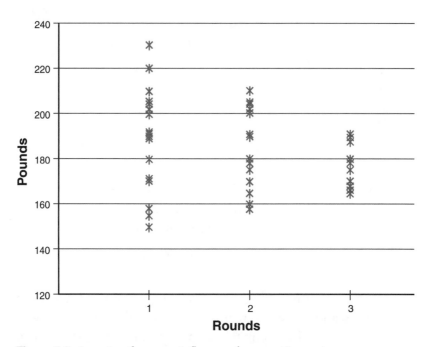

Figure 5.2 *Assessing the group influence of a team: Group A*

It would be naïve for John to assume that this is a dem-onstration of desirable behavior. It is possible that the "center" is not the optimal place to be in all decision mak-ing. The jelly-bean counting and ox weight examples may cause us to assume that the center is always accurate; how-ever, many other factors can influence the group consen-sus.

The plot depicting the behavior of Group B (see Figure 5.3) demonstrates a different outcome. Most members of the group are stubbornly sticking with their original guess-es. It's possible that some members of the group won't allow themselves to be influenced and drawn away from their own opinions. If John were leading a group like this, he should plan on spending much more time monitoring decision making. It's probable with a group like this that there can be a lot of arguments and debates about even the most trivial decisions. Because the members of this group demonstrated that they are unyielding on something as unimportant as guessing weight, they are likely to drag out conversations about more important project-related topics.

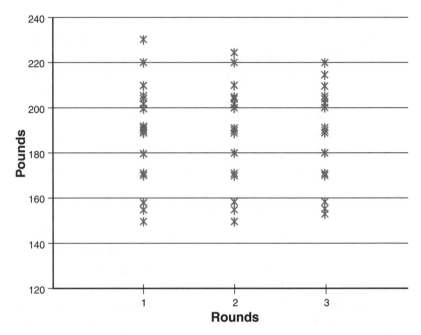

Figure 5.3 *A different outcome: Group B*

Six Degrees of the Perfect Ice Cream Sundae

Late one Saturday night while watching a movie with Mary, John developed a craving for an ice cream sundae. After John clicked pause and announced his craving, Mary offered to build sundaes for both of them. Mary asked John what he wanted on his sundae. John was very particular about his ice cream sundaes, and he took pause before acknowledging Mary's offer. Mary had never made a sundae for John before, and even if he provided a list of the ingredients he wanted, there was no way that Mary would know John's preferences for quantities and layering of those ingredients.

Although John didn't want to scoff at Mary's kind offer to make a sundae for him, he realized that it would be so much easier to go to the kitchen and make it himself. Imagine the same scenario with one added degree of communication: John provided his requirements to Mary, who then went to the ice cream shop. At the ice cream shop, Mary gave John's requirements to the teenager behind the counter. Imagine if the clerk behind the counter wrote down the ice cream sundae instructions and handed it to yet another person to create the sundae. Each additional participant in the sundae-making process introduces additional opportunities for John's requirements to be misapplied.

Software projects are usually far too complex to be accomplished by one individual. To add to this complexity, it's one thing for John to create the perfect ice cream sundae for himself, and it is yet another thing altogether to create the perfect ice cream sundae to satisfy the requirements of a large group of people. Specialized skills and the quantity of work favor the need for multiple participants in the process. As the number of participants increases, there is an increased likelihood of differences of opinion on the team.

What should John have done? The only way John can truly get the sundae he wanted was to participate directly in the process of sundae building. Anything else introduces risk that he will not get what he wants. The same holds true on agile project teams. This illustrates why stakeholder involvement is key to the success of projects.

Diametrically Opposing Forces

In Taoist philosophy, the concept of yin and yang describes two diametrically opposing forces. Each of the forces exists independently while at the same time are in opposition to one another. For example, light and dark are opposites. The concept of light would make no sense if it weren't for dark. Thus, dark defines light, and light defines dark. Together, dark and light oppose one another and form a more profound thing that is both dark and light. The symbol for yin and yang is shown in Figure 5.4.

Figure 5.4 *Yin and yang*

Understanding yin yang and its surrounding philosophies can be complex. For the purposes of this book, suffice it to say that yin and yang are opposing, rooted together, transforming each other, and are balanced.

On typical project teams, traditionally there are certain roles played by individuals that have inherent opposition to other roles. Let's call the person funding a project the "product owner," and let's call the person managing the project the "project manager." The product owner seems to be continuously concerned with staying on budget and meeting deadlines, whereas the project manager seems to be concerned with excessive requirements changes and complaints about the productivity of the project team. This conflict can cause frustration and tension between these individuals. At the same time, the conflict cultivates interactions that positively contribute to the success of the project.

It's natural for many individuals to avoid conflict as much as possible. However, certain project role pairings have built-in conflict that play an important part in the dynamics of a high-functioning project team, including the following:

- Business analysis versus business domain experts

- Development versus systems analysis

- Quality assurance versus development

- Project management versus business management

Figure 5.5 further summarizes these relationships.

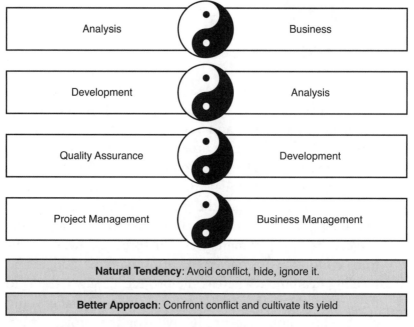

Figure 5.5 *Yin and yang of roles*

In many organizations, the business analyst (BA) role was born out of a business role. Sometimes a BA role begins as a temporary assignment for a major project and evolves into a full-time position in the software development organization. Regardless of where the BA role is found in an organization, the BA is a proxy representative of the business. Over time, however, the authority of the BA can diminish, and the power to make business decisions can be taken away. When this happens, the BA becomes an arbiter of opinions between the project organization and the business domain experts (and the actual business decision makers).

Without the tension normally present when BAs collaborate with business domain experts, the best and most important requirements are unlikely to surface. When BAs and business experts interact, each individual has a different context: background, experiences, opinions, and dogmas. At the intersection of these items for multiple people, both agreement and conflict occur. Through the hassles of arguing, debating, agreeing, and disagreeing, the most important priority requirements are often revealed.

Similarly, developers may clash with domain experts when determining how to implement a solution to a business problem. Developers also tend to have a lot of conflict with those in quality assurance roles. When one of the authors was managing a QA group for a large company, the developers fumed when the daily "Bug Report" was published. After a bit of diplomacy, a compromise was reached, and from that point forward the daily report was renamed the "Findings Report." Regardless of the name, the conflict between the QA and developer roles is engineered to increase the quality of the software being built.

Without all the conflict that occurs when these roles are brought together, quality and productivity would suffer. Some may see the existence of conflict as harming productivity because it takes time away from "production."

However, if conflict were avoided, quality is likely to suffer. Building the wrong thing or building the thing the wrong way is often the result of conflict avoidance.

Closing

Collaboration is costly and time-consuming. It requires much less energy to solve a problem individually than with a group. However, the quality of group performance has been demonstrated time and time again to far exceed individual performance.

When collaborating, it's natural to want to avoid conflict. However, allowing conflict to happen and leveraging the wisdom of the group is likely to lead to higher quality results. The process may take longer, but the savings of delivering the right thing now far exceeds the cost of building the wrong thing with poor quality.

Chapter 6

Behavior and Teams

Now that Lydia got the team to start understanding each other's behaviors and to modify communication styles to work more effectively as a team, the group needed a tool to easily visualize and understand the team dynamics as a whole. The team was ready to learn about and apply lessons learned from "the wheel."

Harmony/Conflict

Chapter 2, "Behavior and Individuals," discussed DISC to understand and accept individuals and to achieve greater communication on a one-on-one basis. This chapter builds on this core understanding and expands it to a team level. The "wheel" plots an entire team on a spatially accurate circle. Although several wheels exist, Figure 6.1 shows an example of a wheel provided by The Abelson Group.

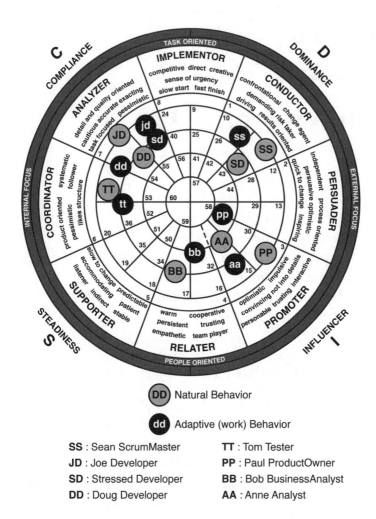

Figure 6.1 *Team Wheel (The Abelson DISC Behaviors Wheel is an adaptation of the Target Training International, LTD. Wheel and is a trademark of The Abelson Group^{TM})*

The wheel is a simple, yet extremely powerful tool applicable to any agile team. The wheel is a true geometric figure; the closer team members are located to each other spatially, the closer their behaviors. The team can visually see how well team members will get along and where to be prepared for natural conflict. Conflict is magnified if some team members have not been trained in DISC.

Based on the location of Joe Developer and Doug Developer in the wheel depicted in Figure 6.1, they should get along extremely well like two peas in a pod. Paul Product Owner and Joe Developer, however, will have a tendency to conflict.

An exercise that could be conducted in a training class is to have students write down the names of three individuals with whom they enjoy their company. Then list three persons that they might detest or not want to hang out with. The three enjoyable individuals typically have similar DISC profiles, and the three detested ones typically have polar opposite profiles (that is, are furthest away from them in the wheel). Many believe this is because people tend to like people who are like themselves. Two I's (influencers) will have lots of conversation; two S's (supporters) may be best friends; two C's (critical thinkers) will thrive on details within the team; but what about two D's (dominators)?

The following is another true story regarding a leader of a consulting company in Dallas. The company wanted someone to move out to Denver to help start a new office. Denver, the mountains, skiing, cooler weather...how could anyone pass that up? It was almost a dream come true when three Principal Consultants volunteered to join the leader and move to Denver to help the start-up office. Principal-level consultants were few and far between because they had a unique combination of the strongest technical skills combined with outstanding communication ability and business acumen to lead teams and help land new business. This supposed dream turned out to be a nightmare.

As you probably expected, these three Principal Consultants were extremely high D's. Because high D's are tremendously competitive, they all strived to be the top dog and the "right-hand man" of the leader of this small, new office. The leader wound up literally facilitating a discussion to help them try to understand and accept each other. He discussed how each was more than capable and had their unique strengths and weaknesses. And he then went on to explain that none of them had to be the top dog because they were a team. Although he never completely solved the problem, the discussion avoided what would have probably resulted in fist fights.

Why Not Hire a Team with Members That Will All Naturally Get Along?

Wouldn't it be best to just hire a team of all C's, all S's or all I's so that everyone would just get along. Unfortunately, that seemingly simple solution simply will not work.

What would happen if you hired a team of all C's? On the positive side, all work would be done with high quality and perfection. On the negative side, however, things would tend to take longer. No one would be naturally driving the project to completion. You may have achieved the prefect product if the project did not get canceled by stakeholders concerned that it was taking too long and costing too much money.

"The Dream Team"

Staffing a team with individual superstars does not always lead to success. The team must work together as a team. Recall the 2002 U.S. national basketball team that finished sixth in the World Championships. After going 58–0 over a period of 10 years with NBA players, this team lost three games and went from being the dream team to a nightmare. A former dream team member, Bill Walton, expressed that there was no dynamic on the court.

So the best teams comprise a blend of behavioral profiles. You want team members to consist of a combination of D's who will make quicker decisions and help drive the project; C's who will focus on the details as they analyze requirements, test, and write code; S's who will bring harmony to the team; and I's who will keep the communication going, optimism high, and energy flowing. It is healthy to have some team members optimistically viewing the project in a "glass is half full" perspective while others are continually concerned about the project's status or level of quality. Therefore the best teams have a mix of behavioral profiles that in turn tends to also result in natural conflict.

Be Prepared for Conflict

The beauty of the wheel is that it immediately visually shows team members where this natural conflict will occur. This is especially important with new teams who have not yet gotten to know one another and who have not gone through the forming, storming, norming, and performing stages as described in Chapter 3, "Team Dynamics."

The more individuals' locations on the wheel is to the outside of the wheel, the more intense their behaviors. So a D on the outskirts of the wheel will tend to be extremely outspoken and driven. She could likely appear to someone who is on the opposite side of the wheel as being arrogant, opinionated, or even rude. A D who is closer to the middle of the wheel will have tendencies to speak up and drive the project, but these behaviors will not appear as intense to others.

Team members can understand and accept one another and know how to best communicate with one another by looking at the wheel. Similarly, they can be prepared for conflict. For example, an I and a C will naturally conflict or at a minimum will naturally annoy one another. The C will want data, whereas the I says "trust me." Similarly, a D will want quick answers, whereas a C will tend to over-analyze (to the D's perspective anyway).

Stressed Out

Will individuals behave differently under stress? That depends. The wheel shows each individual's natural behavior (see the initials in the figure that are uppercase) and their adapted behavior (see the lowercase initials).

You can see that in most cases in the preceding example, the team members' natural and adaptive behaviors are similar. Look closely at Stressed Developer (SD). His natural behavioral profile is a D, but his adaptive behavior is a C. That is, to successfully be a developer in this organization, he has adapted his behavior to that of a C. However, under stress his natural behavior will be revealed.

Team members who naturally seem to get along may all of a sudden become conflicted when the project falls behind schedule and the team feels pressured or when some stakeholder indicates she was not happy with the results of a sprint. Stressed Developer will revert to his natural behavioral tendencies and will start to drive things and be a little more outspoken than he used to be. Without knowledge gained from the wheel, team members may get caught off guard, resulting in clashes and even greater stress on the team.

By viewing the wheel in advance of stressful situations that occur from time to time on projects, the team can be prepared for different behaviors that will surface under stress or pressure.

Fill the Gaps

Another important item that can be gleaned from observing the wheel is gaps on teams. For example, envision a team's wheel displaying no individuals in the D segment of the circle. The team would most likely lack a drive for closure, take longer to make decisions, and have less of a sense of urgency. In this situation, either someone needs to take the role of a D when working on the project, or the team should hire a D. Either way works; however, a team member acting in a role outside of his normal behavioral style may become overly stressed as he works harder trying to behave in a way that conflicts with his natural style.

Organizational or Team Culture

Teams and sometimes entire organizations share a common culture. For example, a large biotech company employed mostly scientists. Even the leaders of the organization were once hands-on scientists. As you might imagine, most individuals at this company were high C's. In general, the company made slow decisions, the employees were low-key and detail-oriented and did not like change.

In another example, at a large finance company, the culture was fast-paced, voicing conflicting opinions was encouraged, and there was frequent change. This company's culture was that of a D.

By observing the wheel of a team or the wheels of many teams within a company, you can depict what the culture will be and gain significant insight on how the team and/or organization will behave.

Closing

The best teams have a blend of behavioral profiles, which also means that the best teams will be up against natural human conflict. Understanding the DISC as a general framework is one step in helping to minimize conflicts. Visually seeing who on the team will likely conflict with whom will best prepare everyone. Doing this at the onset of a project is critical. After conflict occurs and relationships potentially are destroyed, it is too late.

Chapter 7

Change

Lydia was happy that the team had now optimized its interactions. Everyone was aware of the natural and adapted behavioral traits of one another on the team. All team members respected one another and understood why team members behaved the way they did.

Lydia observed another issue. Some members of the team felt less comfortable with the changes associated with their relatively newly adapted agile approach.

A True Story

In early 1984, the headquarters of a large insurance company in Texas was in the throes of email adoption. As with many companies at that time, the promising new technology had a provocative return on investment. Benefits included increased productivity through faster communication, elimination of the typing pools, reduction of secretarial positions, and most significantly—paper savings.

The hundreds of thousands of pages per year that were typed, distributed, read, and discarded would be virtually eliminated. With this new technology, it was possible that paper could completely disappear from the office scene. The business case used to justify buying all the fancy new computing equipment was based completely on the cost savings from less paper.

The implementation team was unprepared for what happened. Although many of the new "office automation" users were enamored with this new toy, many others resisted. Logging into this new system to get access to intra-office communication was tedious, and it was easy to forget to check. The "old way," glancing over at the inbox on the corner of the desk, was more intuitive and efficient. It had been much easier to know if there were a memo to read because it would be there, easily visible inside the inbox.

Because a faction of users resisted using the new electronic mail system, it was useless for others to use it as a reliable way to communicate. It hardly seemed worth the trouble to send someone an email if there were no way to know when and if they would actually see it. Nevertheless, they didn't have a choice because they no longer had secretaries and typists to create memos for them.

For many of those who used the new system, reading memos online was a chore. Because they were so accustomed to reading memos on paper, many of these people printed *every* email. Because the volume of emails was greater than the volume of paper memorandums, paper consumption was an order of magnitude more than before email. The unexpected printing volume thwarted any chance to meet the return on investment goals, based on the original paper savings-based ROI formula.

So why all the fuss? The company made a huge investment in some cool technology that would make everyone's life easier. How could anyone possibly resist? This true story is a great example of the power that change resistance can have on a company, a department, a team, and even individuals. By overlooking the resistance to change, implementation and adoption of the new system became much more laborious and expensive than originally planned.

Project teams adopting new approaches such as agile often encounter resistance as well. This resistance often has no logical or rational basis, yet it can be powerful enough to impede adoption of better, more efficient ways to run a project.

Why Is Change Difficult?

In 1589, Gerardus Mercator created a world map that would forever impact the way the world is viewed. The Mercator Projection flattened the world and significantly skewed proportions of the land masses. For example, the Mercator map greatly exaggerates the size of Alaska, Greenland, and Europe, while at the same time depicts Brazil and Africa as significantly smaller than they actually are (see Figure 7.1).

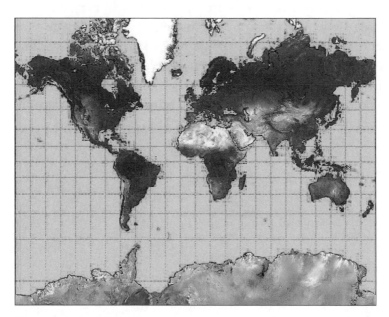

Figure 7.1 *Standard Mercator projection*

Looking at a map based on the Mercator projection, it's not too difficult for most people to pick out the United States, Africa, South America, and China. Put your finger on the map near your home town; then follow a line depicting a trip from your home town to the center of the east coast of Australia.

Your understanding of the map, and our ability to navigate the map, is learned and conditioned over time. The more often you see the standard Mercator map, the more you internalize it as the true representation of the world.

Now, what if the map were turned upside down? Using the map in Figure 7.2, try plotting a line from Los Angeles, California, to London, England. Although those are two well-known cities, most people find this task much more difficult because the map is upside down.

An upside down map isn't as unnatural as it may seem. Most people don't realize that placement of north on the top, and south on the bottom, was an arbitrary decision made by an early mapmaker named Ptolemy. In the first century AD, most geographic areas known to Egyptians such as Ptolemy were in the northern Hemisphere, so he chose to place them on the top of the map. Other mapmakers followed suit, and hence north on the top became a notational convention.

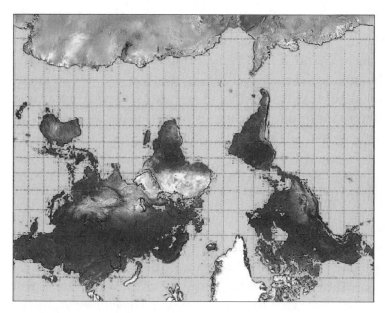

Figure 7.2 *Upside-down Mercator projection*

Over time, Ptolemy's simplistic arbitrary notational convention defined people's visual understanding of geography. If a mapmaker in today's world were to depict a geographic area with north on the bottom and south on the top, the map would be rejected by most people. Adapting to that type of change would be uncomfortable, and the learning curve would be undesirable.

Despite this awareness, many people involved in project work can be ignorant of the effect that change has on others. When building a new system, the software developers' livelihood is based on creating change. At the same time, the world of many users of the new software may resist having to learn new tools.

When Microsoft introduced Office 2007, it made a radical overhaul to the user interface. Microsoft touted these changes as much needed enhancements to the interface, yet many consumers complained about them. "Better" is a relative term, and from the perspective of many consumers, Microsoft did an inadequate job of defining "better."

Process change is unsettling to many as well. Some people may jump at the chance to try a "shiny new" process such as Scrum or eXtreme Programming. Many others, though, will be overwrought with concern about abandoning old skills, developing new skills, extensive learning curves, and reduced positions of power based on years of experience doing things the old way.

Change Squirm

At 9:00 a.m. on Monday morning, Joe walked to the front of the room to launch into his usual kickoff speech for the two-day training class he was about to teach.

Joe started, "Good morning, my name is Joe, and I will be your instructor for *Agile Software Development* for the next two days. It's always a good idea when starting a class for us all to get to know one another." At that point, Joe said nothing. He looked around the room, making eye contact with those students who would permit it. Joe moved from the front of the room to this side and then to the back, continuously paying attention to the students but saying nothing.

After no more than ten seconds, students were already starting to look around at each other. Some made inquisitive gestures, whereas others just looked confused. After a while, a soft murmur started to bubble up from the group, which eventually turned to a smattering of nervous laughter.

Joe created an uncomfortable environment for his students by doing absolutely nothing. In this case, nothing was actually a whole lot. Joe changed the rules without letting anyone know. Those who had ever been in a training class before knew that after his introduction, Joe would likely go around the room and ask people to introduce themselves (or conduct some other form of an interactive ice breaker).

Moments before all this happened, the last of the students had settled into their carefully selected seats, adjusted the seat height, placed their coffee next to their freshly unshrink-wrapped course notebook, and relaxed for a predictable stress-free course introduction.

The silence that Joe created was awkward and painful, and most of the students likely wanted it to end as soon as possible. The awkwardness centered on the uncertainty. Nobody knew what was happening or what was about to happen. This change to conventional expectations put the students outside their comfort zone. You can only imagine their relief when Joe finally broke the silence!

Change Apprehension

Many people dislike change due to fear. Any individual's level of change apprehension is usually due to fear of disruption to core needs. In Chapter 4, "Communication," a depiction of these core needs was shown using Maslow's Hierarchy of Needs. Using that model, you can recognize that at the tip of the hierarchy, changes (or anticipated changes) to those needs can cause apprehension. As you move down the hierarchy to the basic needs, the apprehension increases by orders of magnitude (see Figure 7.3).

Figure 7.3 *Impact of change related to the Hierarchy of Needs*

Fear of Changes to Self-Actualization Needs

This level of the hierarchy is focused on people's needs related to how their job functions, roles, and responsibilities may be affected by the change.

Individuals who enjoy a high level of creativity in their job may stress about a change that is going to restrict their creative outlet. Perhaps the introduction of a new highly prescriptive process will remove their ability to make spontaneous decisions about what should be done and when.

An accomplished painter would be uncomfortable if required to paint using a paint-by-numbers kit. Similarly, individuals who are motivated by their ability to solve problems creatively and autonomously will be uncomfortable when told to step in alignment and follow a structured process.

The reverse situation is also true: individuals who prefer following a prescriptive step-by-step process when told to rely more on intuition, experience, and instinct.

Fear of Changes to Esteem Needs

When introducing process changes, there can often be an impact to organizational status. Those who like managing other people may fear a change to a flatter organization in which supervisor/subordinate roles are shuffled around. A seemingly subtle change can cause undue stress to some individuals: changes to job titles. Many individuals work for years to climb the ladder of job titles, and to some, the title can be more valuable than a corresponding salary increase. This is especially true when these individuals' workplace motivators are individualistic/political (see Chapter 8, "Motivators," for more details).

When a Scrum coach announces to a new agile team that all former titles are going away and will be replaced by these fancy new titles, this can be perceived by some as stripping away stripes that were earned over years of sweat and loyalty. A cavalier pronouncement of the abandonment of job titles can cause a great degree of stress for members of a team.

Fear of Changes to Love/Belonging Needs

At the Love/Belonging level the initial instinct is to think of family and loved ones. Certainly any change that can have an impact on the quality of family life can cause fear and stress.

Beyond family, many sociological units exist within a company that individuals may fear being separated from. When reorganizations happen and new project teams are formed, many thoughts will run through individuals' heads, such as the following:

- Will they like me?

- Will I have someone to eat lunch with?

- Will somebody on the team be interested in talking about my Fantasy Football team with me?

Fear of Changes to Safety Needs

Any change that can cause concern about job security and continued employability fall into this category. Even if management states that training and time for reskilling will be provided, the fear may still often be present. The only certainties related to an employee's skills are those already present. There is never a guarantee that new skills can and will be acquired and honed in a timely manner.

John the project manager, who worked hard to earn his Project Management Professional (PMP™) designation, was told that he will now be a ScrumMaster. Further, he was told by an agile consultant that his "old school" project management skills are no longer useful. Whether that statement is true or not, John may develop fear at multiple levels. He may fear loss of his job if he doesn't do well in the new role, which carries with it changes to the relationships he has developed with his colleagues, loss of esteem by having his title stripped away, and loss of job responsibilities that he enjoys doing.

Fear of Changes to Physiological Needs

The base of the needs hierarchy, those fundamental needs that stand above all, includes the needs for food, water, sleep, air, and so on. Pure human instinct ought to be enough to ensure that these needs are met. Some may think that they can't be affected by change in the workplace. However, that's not the case.

When new project teams are formed and new processes are introduced, often some individuals will worry about changes to their eating and sleeping cycles. When the eager new ScrumMaster announces that the daily standup meetings will be held at 7:30 every morning so that "We can launch every day bright and early on the right foot," it's bound to be met with resistance.

James may complain that this interferes with taking his child to school, which could be accommodated as a valid reason. However, Mary has a productive sleep cycle that would be disrupted if she had to get to work before 9:00 a.m. Although James' excuse may be seen as valid, Mary's may be scoffed at as trivial. Coming in an hour and a half earlier could completely disrupt Mary's productivity and mood.

Change Coach

An experienced individual such as a consultant can be brought onto the team to coach the members through the change process.

Many coaches in the marketplace tout their skills in agile software development, which can qualify them to be good coaches. When hiring a coach, you also need to assess the coach's skills at managing individual and team changes. A good coach is skillful at identifying and addressing the many fears of change so that they don't stand in the way of advancing the project forward.

Imagine Jenny's boss Fred noticing that she seems to have self-confidence issues. Is it advisable for Fred to give Jenny a book titled *How to Improve your Self-Esteem*? Certainly it's possible, and ethical, and maybe even appropriate to some. However, is it advisable? Self-help is usually only effective when it is self-driven.

In the same spirit as not handing someone a self-help book, an effective coach helps an individual understand and rationalize barriers to change so that they can be removed.

Change Catalyst

Change in the overall dynamics and behavior of a team can change as a result of one individual's behavior. When the team captain of a losing basketball team steps up his game while encouraging everyone else to do the same, he can positively affect the behavior of everyone on the team. If another team member who isn't in a leadership role were to do the same thing, it could still potentially boost the productivity of the rest of the members of the team.

In business, inserting a highly productive person on a team has the capability of positively affecting other team members' productivity. Some may follow suit out of shame or competition or perhaps just out of respect or admiration for the positive role model.

The role model can work against the desired goals of a team as well. It's also possible for the behavior of an entire team to be negatively influenced by one team member. Dr. William Felps from the University of Washington Business School ran an experiment in which he assembled groups to solve a problem together. Felps assembled groups of individuals to participate in a problem solving exercise. One participant was a "plant"—a confederate trained by Felps to behave a specific way.

In the first group, the confederate behaved in a manner that Felps labeled interpersonal deviance, which is referred to as the "jerk." The jerk was quick to dismiss others' ideas for solving the problem, yet he didn't offer concrete solutions of his own.

In the second group, the confederate withheld effort and is referred to as the "slacker." The slacker showed little interest in the problem-solving exercise and leaned back in his chair with his feet up on the table while texting on his cell phone.

In the last group, the confederate showed affective negativity, or the "depressive." He told the group that his cat just died and took on the appearance of a person in despair. He expressed doubt that the group could succeed at the unpleasant exercise.

When conducting this experiment, Felps found that the confederate's toxic behavior became contagious; it catalyzed negative behavior across the team. The confederate's jerk behavior begets jerk behavior by others on the team, and the same was true for the slacker and the depressive. The negative effect of the bad apple drove down the rate of success on the problem being solved.

Negative behavior has a more profound emulating affect on a group than positive behavior. In other words, team members are more likely to adopt the behavior of a negative individual than they are to adopt the behavior of a positive individual.

It may not be possible to eliminate bad-apple behavior completely. Although some individuals may regularly exhibit negative behavior, it's possible for any or all team members to behave negatively on any given day. Therefore, to avoid the bad-apple effect, it's best when the team maintains conscious awareness of the effect so that it can expose it and shut it down when it appears. This may sound good on paper but requires a highly mature and self-aware team.

Tracing to the Roots

Most current pop, rock, and jazz songs last approximately three minutes, more or less. For years, the music industry was built around that parameter. Why not ten minutes, or five minutes, or one minute? How was it decided that three minutes was the default duration of a single?

In the early 1900s, most recordings were sold on seven-inch 78 rpm discs. The groove on these discs could hold a recording up to three minutes and five seconds. To sell a song, a musician was constrained to this time limit.

Modern recording and music distribution technologies have eliminated the physical constraint of the length of a song. Nevertheless, the music industry has grown up around the notion that a single is three to four minutes long. Some artists deviate, of course, but most single track recordings still conform to that arbitrary constraint. If a new artist were to release a series of six-minute songs, it's probable that listeners would notice that they are unusually long. When things become a certain way, it's difficult to change even if the original purpose no longer exists.

Grass Roots Resistance to Change

Often a process, system, or organizational structure has passed its reason for being long ago. Nevertheless, changing or eliminating it can be an uphill battle. When routines become habit, and habits become comfortable, change or elimination can become seemingly impossible.

Recall the upside-down map from the beginning of the chapter. Putting the northern hemisphere on the bottom of a map is certainly possible; however, widespread adoption of that change would be an extraordinary undertaking, even if everyone agreed that Ptolemy's decision to put north on the top was an arbitrary one.

The approximate calendar used by most schools in the United States begins in late August or early September and continues until late May or early June. This was originally established in the nineteenth century in rural areas to enable children to be home to work in the fields during the summer. About the same time, wealthy families in big cities pressed for longer vacation periods in the summer so that they could escape the heat of the city.

There have been efforts in recent years by some school districts to change to a year-round school calendar with breaks distributed throughout the year. A goal of the year-round calendar is to provide students with seamless continuity from one grade to the next.

In 1991, Northside School District in San Antonio, Texas, was one of many school districts in the United States that introduced a pilot year-round school program. The program was deemed a success by the families that had volunteered to participate in the pilot. The two-week break in October was touted as a great benefit because family vacations were possible while the weather was still nice but the crowds were gone.

When the school district tried expanding the program beyond the pilot, however, it was met with tremendous resistance from parent groups. Many of the complaints were based on logistical concerns such as arranging childcare during several short breaks versus one long break. The primary reason most objected, however, was resistance to change. Elimination of the traditionally long summer vacation was perceived as too dramatic a shift from what people were used to.

Although some year-round school programs still exist, most were abandoned. The force of resistance was far too great for the resources of most school districts to contend with. The introduction of change in companies often can also be met with frustration and great forces of resistance.

Pushing change from the top-down is always certainly possible, but in the face of that, grass roots resistance can block change. Change can be imposed, but it may not accomplish its goals if there is sufficient force working against it. For this reason, pushing change from the top-down should be complemented with acceptance and support from the bottom-up as well.

Exposing the Origins

When encouraging change in the face of a fear of change, it can be helpful to expose the origins of the conventional processes. Just as the school calendar was based on expired needs, many processes in business were conceived based on traditional requirements that are no longer valid.

Many traditional project managers use a Gantt chart to depict the project plan. The Gantt chart was developed by Henry Gantt in 1910. The first major project to use it was the construction of the Hoover Dam. For years, Gantt charts were used for managing construction projects—many decades before the existence of software projects. Many of the earliest software project management processes were based on processes that had been used to construct buildings and roadways.

Building software, particularly with current-day tools, differs greatly from building and roadway construction projects. Building construction projects usually require comprehensive planning and design before actual construction can begin. On software projects, however, creative choice during construction is permissible and actually results in software that better meets customer needs.

For most, Gantt charts are hard not to like. They align well with the way most people think about organizing work. Consider the following example of the tasks involved in a family cleaning a house:

Clean the kitchen.
- Clean the oven.
- Clean the dishes.
- Clean the refrigerator.
- Clean the floor.
- Clean the counters.

Clean the family room.
- Vacuum the floor.
- Dust the furniture.

- Vacuum the sofa.
- Clean carpet stains.

And so on...

Sequence matters for some of these tasks because they depend on other tasks having already happened, whereas others could be done at any time. Say you have four workers: Joe, Tim, Nikki, and Danni. By assigning these workers to specific tasks, you could lay out a neat plan for getting the house cleaned in a quick efficient manner.

Some days, this plan could be executed flawlessly with a high degree of predictability. At other times, it could fail miserably. Perhaps a worker gets sick, or the vacuum cleaner breaks, or the carpet has grape juice stains that require additional effort to remove.

Projects with a high degree of creative choice, however, don't usually work well by following a prescriptive step-by-step serial plan. Choices of what tasks to do and when to do them is often more spontaneous than in the house cleaning example. Tasks are determined based on recently completed work. Those who have grown up in the Gantt world may have a difficult time accepting any other way of organizing work.

Using Gantt charts to run a software development project could be analogous to using a riding mower to cultivate a flower garden. Nevertheless, Gantt charts continue to be used on software projects despite the introduction of better tools for managing projects iteratively. Yes, change certainly is difficult.

Exercise

In Chapter 15, "Change Exercise," you can find an exercise that creates a fun, safe environment to openly discuss things that require changing. The facilitator should carefully read this chapter and the workshop instructions before diving into this exercise, more so than any of the other exercises in this book. Change can cause hot flashes and cold sweats, and it's important for the facilitator to keep an observant eye out for signs of resistance and to be prepared to address that resistance when it surfaces.

Closing

Aversion to change is inherent in most people. Even a person who is a catalyst for change (a change agent) may resist when others attempt to impose changes of their own. This phenomenon makes it difficult for organizations and teams to adapt to better ways of working together on projects.

A step in the right direction is to accept that change is difficult for most people. This can help overcome frustration with those who resist change. The change exercise in Chapter 15 of this book offers a tool that you can use to expose those areas needing change so that they can be addressed head-on.

Chapter 8

Motivators

The team was now performing as an agile team with high bandwidth communication, self-organization, collaboration, and teamwork. To ensure everyone maintained the highest level of motivation, Lydia wanted to find out more information regarding what motivated each member of the team. This way she and the team could best ensure each individual on the project remained satisfied.

This chapter discusses three factors that influence the motivation of team members:

- Individual workplace motivators

- Leveraging personal strengths

- Leadership and environment

Individual Workplace Motivators

DISC explains how people will behave. Workplace motivators explain why they behave as they do. As mentioned in Chapter 2, "Behaviors and Individuals," if you master understanding DISC you can often tell a person's behavioral profile just by observing their body language combined with the way the person communicates. Motivators are different. You cannot tell what motivates a person just by observation. They are therefore often referred to as "hidden motivators."

Similar to how DISC indicates that everyone has a blend of four behaviors, workplace motivators indicates that everyone has a blend of six motivators. But the dominant motivators drive why they do things.

Resource

Types of Men: The Psychology and Ethics of Personality, Eduard Spranger, 1928.

Some of the DISC providers also offer motivator assessments. The following paragraphs describe the six motivators that comprise the blend.

Theoretical

Individuals who rank high for the theoretical motivator have a need for learning. They have a passion for knowledge and discovery of truth. They love ideas, explore new interests, and have a desire to learn about almost anything. They seek to observe and reason.

Utilitarian/Economic

Some providers of motivation assessments call this category the economic motivator, and others call it utilitarian. Regardless of the category name, people who have a high score in this category have a need for practicality, utility, and financial gain. They tend to feel more secure when they have and accumulate tangible wealth. They often have a drive to feel financially secure in later years. They want what is useful, practical, and efficient.

Aesthetic

Those who score high in the aesthetic category have a tendency to appreciate beauty, nature, the environment, pleasant surroundings, unity, and balance. They continually search for beauty and harmony in everything they do. They are typically highly aware of their inner feelings and their surroundings. They value the environments where they work and live and have a desire to experience new things, activities, and places.

Social

Socially motivated individuals have a need to help others. They may even have a passion to help others and feel fulfilled when they succeed. They are less concerned about profit than for the needs of others. They tend to sacrifice their own needs for the needs of others and to help others.

Individualistic/Political

Some providers of motivation assessments call this category individualistic, and others call it political. Individuals strong in this category tend to have a need for personal power, influence, and fame. They have a desire and a passion to be at the top of an organization. Title is important. They have a passion to control others: people, money, assets, and so on. They like having responsibility, individually and within the team.

Traditional/Regulatory

Depending on the provider, this category is called either traditional or regulatory. People who rank high in this category tend to have an interest in rules, unity, order, and tradition. They believe in structure; there is a right and a wrong way to do things. They have a passion to search for the highest meaning of life and look for rules to guide their behaviors. They typically live by a set of standards or a belief system and encourage others to also embrace these rules/beliefs. They like to have rules and regulations and to do things "by the book."

Why Is This Important?

In DISC, there are no good or bad behavioral profiles; people are just different. The same goes for motivators. There are no right or wrong motivators. It is simply that people are wired differently, and what motivates one person may not motivate another.

Individuals perform best when they are in roles and environments that leverage what motivates them. For example, if people are highly motivated by learning (the theoretical motivator) and are on a project or team where there is no opportunity to learn, they will not be satisfied, will most likely experience some stress because of this, and may eventually quit.

Knowing each member of the team's motivators can help team members perform tasks or do things that match their needs whenever possible. As examples, have a theoretically motivated individual lead efforts on analyzing a new technology required for the project; allow the aesthetically motivated person to sit in the cube by the window; have the politically motivated person integrate the newly acquired organization into the team. Because agile teams are self-organizing, it is valuable for team members to know one another's workplace motivators in order to be cognizant of each other's needs.

Work can change from "work" to "fun" when the job closely matches and satisfies a person's motivations or needs.

Strategies for Motivating

Table 8.1 provides examples of strategies for motivating others depending on their motivational profiles.

Table 8.1 *Strategies for Motivating*

Motive	Strategies for Motivating
Theoretical	Give them activities to learn and discover; ask them questions; challenge them to demonstrate why they are correct about something.
Economic/ Utilitarian	Give them opportunities for financial advancement; effectively use their time; give them something in return for what they contribute.
Aesthetic	Give them a pleasant work environment; allow them to express their thoughts and ideas.
Social	Give them opportunities to help others; help them understand their true value because it is more important than they think. (They tend to undervalue their services and give them away to others.)
Individualistic/ Political	Give them opportunities to lead others and to set/enforce the rules; Allow them to be visionaries and work toward achieving those visions.
Traditional/ Regulatory	Give them structure and guidelines to follow that fall within their principles/rules/belief system.

As a real-world example, there was a senior vice president (SVP) in a company in the financial services domain that was under stress because he had promised a critical system would be complete by a certain date but was behind schedule. He therefore told the team to work nights and weekends to ensure the project was completed on time. He gave an incentive to the project manager by telling him that he would be promoted to a vice president (VP) if the project were implemented on time. Similarly, he attempted to motivate the developers by offering a financial bonus if the date were achieved. Now, aside from violating many agile principals by not maintaining a sustainable pace; by promising an arbitrary project end date to stakeholders;

and by telling the team what to do in a command-and-control like manner, there were additional flaws in the SVP's actions. It turned out that the PM was not actually motivated by a VP title because his individualistic/political component was one of his least important motivators. Moreover, the majority of the development team was motivated mostly by the theoretical motive, and most had a low economic motivator.

At first the motivation of an increase of money was appealing to some of the team members. But as the project dragged on longer and longer, and as many nights and weekends were required, the project began to unravel further and was unsuccessful at the end. Even if the members were motivated by these incentives, it still would likely have failed in this particular case. But one interesting observation from this experience was that most individuals tend to assume that the motivations of others match their own. The SVP, who was highly motivated by title and money, assumed everyone else must be. He did not realize that people are wired differently.

Somewhat similar to the concept of a DISC wheel discussed in Chapter 6, "Behavior and Teams," some workplace motivator providers supply a "wheel" of workplace motivators for a team. Figure 8.1 shows an example of a wheel, provided by The Abelson Group. The team members' top motivators are shown in the center circle, their second highest motivators in the second circle, and least passionate motivators in the outer circle.

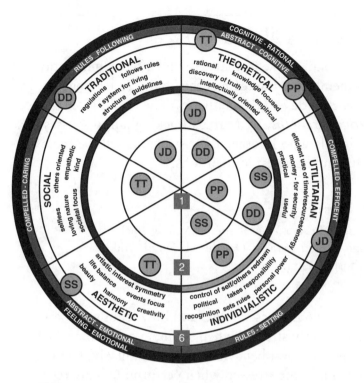

1 Most Passionate

2 Second Most Passionate

6 Least Passionate

SS : Sean ScrumMaster
PP : Paul ProductOwner
JD : Joe Developer
DD : Doug Developer
TT : Tom Tester

Figure 8.1 *Team Motivators Wheel—The Abelson Values/Motives/ Work-Related-Passions Wheel™ is an adaptation of the Target Training International, LTD. Motives Wheel and is a trademark of The Abelson Group™.*

The wheel provides a simple visual representation to quickly view the workplace motivators of every team member and to also observe similarities within the team.

Leveraging Strengths

The second element that greatly affects motivation of each member of the team is the ability to leverage natural strengths in day-to-day activities. The book, *Now Discover Your Strengths,* by Marcus Buckingham discusses how individuals who leverage their strengths will be most successful and happiest in their jobs.

Resource

Now, Discover Your Strengths, Marcus Buckingham and Donald O. Clifton, Simon and Schuster, 2001.

Chapter 6 discussed DISC and how team members may become overly stressed when acting in a role that conflicts with their natural behavioral styles. Similarly, team members can become stressed when performing daily responsibilities that do not align with their natural strengths. As a real-world example, a colleague was asked to play a role in a desk job writing architectural design documentation when his core strength was communicating with people. His greatest strength and most successful roles performed in the past were those of a coach, mentor, instructor, and change agent. When playing the role of an architect however, he was exhausted at the end of each day and eventually became burnt out on the job. Needless to say, he was quite unhappy while playing this role.

Understanding your team members' strengths and having everyone perform tasks that best use these strengths can result in the highest performing teams and the most motivated team members.

Leadership and Environment

Even if individuals work in jobs that align with both their workplace motivators and strengths, it is also critical to work in a good environment that fosters respect and autonomy in order to remain highly motivated. An applicable quote comes from Patrick M. Lencioni's book, *The Five Dysfunctions of a Team*, where he says, "Not finance. Not strategy. Not technology. It is teamwork that remains the ultimate competitive advantage, both because it is so powerful and so rare." It is amazing to see companies spend millions of dollars on technologies and tools to enable a competitive advantage. Yet treating people with respect and fostering an environment of teamwork and empowerment costs nothing and is probably the most powerful thing any company or team can do to enable success.

Resource
The Five Dysfunctions of a Team, Patrick M. Lencioni, Jossey-Bass, 2002.

Command-and-control management is the antithesis of agile. Therefore, this is not an issue on agile projects. Right? Unfortunately, the majority of agile projects report into some hierarchy somewhere in the chain of command within the company. A common problem is when an agile project reports to a command-and -control manager.

The following is a true story. Two sprints into an agile project, the director called the ScrumMaster into his office and asked, "Can you explain why this agile project is so successful when we have tried agile in the past and it has never really worked?" In response, the ScrumMaster discussed many of the differences in the mechanics being employed currently versus what the company had done in the past. The discussion ranged from the task board where everyone could visually see the current project status, to the way they ran their daily standup meetings, to the demonstrations held every sprint. By the end of the project, however, the ScrumMaster realized the real answer to the director's question.

The entire management team of this organization was deeply entrenched in a command-and-control culture. It was a common occurrence that the managers would demand and expect everyone to work the weekend and to work after 5 p.m. each day. (One manager was even known to "walk the halls" each day at 5 p.m. to see if everyone was still there.) Also the managers would rarely explain any rationale to the team regarding decisions. These managers would not be part of the solution but would just tell people what to do and often made what appeared to be unreasonable requests.

Not only did some of this behavior violate the agile principal of "a sustainable pace," but also some of the things this management team would say and the way it treated individuals was bordering on abuse. Many employees would refer to the managers as bullies, and several said they were in fear of losing their jobs. Although this extreme behavior is not common, it is common to have some elements of traditional command-and-control behavior within a company. And this behavior is one of the most common factors leading to the detriment of agile adoption or success on individual agile projects.

Closing

DISC explains *how* people will behave, and workplace motivators explains *why* they behave as they do. Everyone has a blend of six workplace motivators, but the dominant motivators drive why they do things. Individuals perform best when they are in roles and environments that leverage what motivates them.

The book *Now Discover Your Strengths* by Marcus Buckingham contains a code where readers can take an online assessment to discover their top strengths. Understanding and leveraging these strengths can result in the highest performing teams and motivated team members.

Agile is about good leadership. A good leader trusts and empowers his team. For individuals to maintain a high degree of motivation, it is important that they also have a relatively high degree of autonomy. Command-and-control managers will hopefully read this chapter, reflect on their own behaviors, and subsequently change.

PART II

Workshop

Chapter 9

Team Dynamics Workshop

As a result of Lydia's hard work, Nathan's team was transformed from a bunch of individuals to a high-performance team. So Nathan decided to put together a team workshop to enable future teams at Autonomous Securities, LLC to quickly learn all these valuable lessons.

Preparation

This book contains all the materials needed to facilitate and run the workshop, with the exception of the following:

- Supplies for the Bridge exercise are inexpensive and can be purchased at a drugstore or grocery store.

- Certain exercises (as described next) require paper, pens, flip charts, whiteboards, index cards, and so on, which most companies have available, but the facilitator needs to be prepared with these supplies.

Workshop Instructions

The Agile Team Dynamics workshop is a powerful way to begin the process of coaching a team toward productivity optimization. The workshop provides a way for team members to learn new skills while learning about each other. Therefore, to get the most value from the time spent participating in the workshop, it's best when a project team attends the workshop together.

The workshop instructions are split into three parts:

- Pre-Workshop
- The Workshop
- Post-Workshop

Pre-Workshop

A day or two prior to the workshop, all participants should complete the DISC assessment and bring their results to the workshop. Many of the workshop exercises and discussions leverage the DISC profile of the participants. From a logistics standpoint, getting all participants to complete the DISC assessment at least one day before the workshop may be the most challenging task of the entire workshop! Participants who show up on the day of the workshop without a completed DISC can disrupt the experience for everyone else, so the facilitator is encouraged to pester everyone with reminders in the days leading up to the workshop.

Do the following:

1. Select a date, location, and times for the workshop. Choose a date when all members of a team are available to attend together. When selecting a room for the workshop, be mindful that the Bridge exercise

requires that the participants be split into groups of 4–6 people, and each group needs a space with two desks or tables separated by three feet. This exercise may not work in a typical conference room, and it may not work in classrooms where the furniture can't be moved. If you can't find a room that works, you may be able to bring in small rolling file cabinets or other similar pieces of furniture that can serve as the surfaces required for building the bridge. All the other workshop exercises can work in any type of room.

2. Have every participant take a DISC assessment prior to the workshop and bring their reports to the workshop. The free DISC contained in this book will suffice for all the exercises other than the BalderDISC exercise found in Chapter 13, "BalderDISC." The BalderDISC exercise requires all participants to take a DISC assessment from a provider that provides a detailed DISC report and a wheel (as opposed to a simple DISC graph). It is therefore important that you plan this well in advance.

3. Make plans for lunch. The Moon exercise is planned to be run during lunchtime, and there is no additional time budgeted for leaving to get food. Ask participants to bring a bag lunch or plan to have lunch brought in during the midpoint of the workshop.

4. Prepare the following materials that will be required during the workshop exercises:

The Bridge
- Drinking straws (three boxes/bags per group)
- Scotch tape (two rolls per group)
- Elastic bands (three small bags or one large bag per group)
- Paper clips (four boxes per group)

Moon Survival

- There are several handouts for this exercise in Chapter 12, "Moon Survival." It's important that participants not look ahead when participating in this exercise. You may choose to bookmark specified pages and instruct the participants not to look ahead, or you may find it easier to copy those pages and distribute them as they are needed during the exercise.

Origami

- There is an origami instruction sheet in Chapter 10, "Communication Origami." Only half the participants will use this instruction sheet. As with Moon Survival, you may choose to copy the instruction sheet ahead of time and hand it out to select participants at the appropriate time. For this exercise you also need a blank sheet of 8½ x 11-inch paper for the other half of the participants.

The Workshop

The workshop lasts approximately eight and a half hours when conducted in the following format. The instructions for all workshop exercises are included in this book. The starting/ending times for each segment can be adjusted if necessary. The times shown in Table 9.1 enable you to run the workshop between 8:30 a.m. and 5:00 p.m. with an exercise during lunch.

Table 9.1 *Workshop Times and Activities*

Time	Activity
8:30–8:45	**Introductions**
	Only 15 minutes is budgeted for introductions. The workshop is all about getting to know each other on several levels. The obligatory "Let's go around the room and each tell something about yourself" exercise is unnecessary at this point and would waste valuable time.
	Instead, use this time to set expectations for the day. These guidelines are recommended to ensure that everyone participates 100% for the entire workshop. If anyone misses all or part of the workshop, it can diminish the value for everyone.
	Do you have your DISC assessment results?
	Plan to work through lunch. There will be short breaks between some of the exercises. Please don't stray too far and return on time.
8:45–9:15	**Communication Origami**
	The origami exercise is a great way to start the day. It energizes the room and gets everyone prepared for a day of highly engaging interactive learning. The origami exercise puts everyone on the same plane because everyone in the room has the same degree of participation.
	When setting up for this exercise, everyone in the room must be paired up with a partner. One member of each pair needs access to the origami instructions found at the end of Chapter 10, but don't allow them to view the instructions until told to do so. The other member of each pair should be given a blank sheet of 8½ x 11-inch paper.
	Follow the facilitation instructions carefully so that the participants fully experience the learning objectives. Spend approximately 5 minutes setting up, 10 minutes folding, and 15 minutes discussing the results. The facilitation instructions describe helpful discussion points. It's helpful to study those prior to running the exercise.

Time	Activity
9:15–9:25	**The Bridge—Introduction** Introduce the Bridge exercise. Be careful not to give away too much information. Most of the learning in this exercise is discovered while the participants are building their bridges, so it's important not to expose the learning objectives ahead of time. As facilitator, read the Bridge instructions in Chapter 11, "Bridge Building," thoroughly ahead of time. Make sure you fully understand the learning objectives and be observant for examples of behavior to discuss after the timed portion of the exercise is complete. While describing the exercise, move furniture (if necessary) and hand out a set of materials to each group. Let everyone know that the "project" will be rigorously timed; they will have 20 minutes to build their bridges.
9:25–9:45	**The Bridge—Project** As stated in the instructions, with little fanfare and a brief introduction, say, "You have 20 minutes to build a bridge between two tables three feet apart that will hold the weight of a book. One, two, three, go!" Follow the facilitation instructions for guidance on things to watch for and when to insert the scripted interjections.
9:45–10:05	**The Bridge—Discussion** See Chapter 11 for post-exercise discussion recommendations.
10:05–10:20	**Break**
10:20–10:30	**Moon Survival—Introduction** Describe the Moon Survival exercise without giving away too many details. Read through the material in Chapter 12 and follow the facilitation instructions. There are multiple handouts for this exercise that must each be distributed at the proper time. To make the most efficient use of time, this exercise can be run during lunch. Participants will be reading and writing during the first part of the exercise, so it's best to choose food that is easy to eat while working.
10:30–10:45	**Moon Survival—Individual Exercise** The exercise has two parts. Each person completes the first part alone for approximately 15 minutes.

Time	Activity
10:45–11:30	**Moon Survival—Group Exercise**
	Without delay, break the room into groups and perform the group exercise in approximately 40 minutes. Some participants may get chatty and interfere with the group's ability to complete this exercise quickly, so the facilitator should keep on top of the time and urge everyone to keep it moving.
11:30–11:45	**Break; lunch setup**
11:45–12:30	**Moon Survival—Discussion (during lunch)**
	The Moon Survival instructions in Chapter 12 provide recommendations for facilitating the post-exercise discussion. In addition to reinforcing the wisdom of crowds, this can be a good opportunity to refer back to their DISC profiles.
12:30-12:45	**BalderDISC Setup**
	Each individual reviews his own detailed DISC report, highlights the sentences he believes most accurately reflect who he is, and creates index cards as described in Chapter 13. To save time, the facilitator could ask the team to perform this setup prior to the start of the workshop.
12:45-1:45	**BalderDISC (team communication)—Exercise**
	Depending on the size of the team and level of discussion that occurs while playing the game, this section could take longer or shorter than one hour. Assuming you have a ten-person team, and assuming you limit each member's discussion to six minutes, this discussion would take one hour. If you have a larger team, you can save time by having the members highlight their DISC reports in advance of the meeting, or you could shorten the time to less than six minutes per person.
1:45-2:15	**BalderDISC (team communication) Post-Exercise Discussion**
	See Chapter 13 for post-exercise discussion recommendations.
2:15–2:30	**Break**

Time	Activity
2:30–2:35	**Assessing Concordance Discordance—Introduction**
	Be sure that the facilitator is willing to expose his/ her weight to the group. Otherwise, choose a different facilitator and/or a different measurable attribute. Prior to starting this exercise, be sure to have three blank slips of paper and a pen available per participant. Prepare the blank weight plot so that it may be revealed with plotted data during each of the three rounds of the exercise. This could be done on a white board or on a spreadsheet, or simply plotted on a piece of paper passed around the room.
2:35–2:45	**Assessing Concordance Discordance—Exercise**
	Follow the instructions in Chapter 14, "Assessing Concordance Discordance." It's important to do each round without revealing who guessed what weights and to have no further explanation or instruction between the three rounds. After finishing three rounds, discuss the results with the group.
2:45–3:00	**Assessing Concordance Discordance—Discussion**
	See Chapter 14 for post-exercise discussion recommendations. Remember that the point of the exercise is to better understand the magnitude of influence members of the group have on one another. When discussing the conformance profile of the group, it's best to accept the behavioral tendencies of the group and focus the conversation on how to operate most productively because of (or despite) what the profile indicates.
3:00–3:10	**Change—Introduction**
	Decide how many teams will be competing and designate a space for each team to work. Have a flip chart or white board available for each team to draw on and a marker or pen. Have a stack of 3x5 cards available. (Assume 5–10 cards per participant.)
	Explain the game to the team following the instructions in Chapter 15, "Change Exercise," and give 5 minutes for each person to fill out the cards. Collect all the cards and mix them up for use during the exercise.

Time	Activity
3:10–3:55	**Change—Exercise** For each round, the facilitator will pick a card off the pile and read the name on the back of the card. This person will come up to the front of the room and help the facilitator monitor this round. Have each team select one person to be the drawer for the round. Follow the instructions in Chapter 15 and ensure that everyone has a chance to participate as a drawer and as a guesser. When someone makes a correct guess, a point is earned for that team, and the round ends. The facilitator should determine how to end the game. Often a time limit or a specified number of rounds is used.
3:55–4:15	**Change—Discussion** Be sure to have a white board or flip chart available to draw the target. See Chapter 15 for facilitating this part of the exercise. The facilitator should be prepared to delicately handle changes that cause discomfort for some. Additionally, there may be disagreements that require some mediation.
4:15–4:30	**Break**
4:30–4:35	**Groups and Decisions—Introduction** Have everyone sit in quadrants of the room in accordance with their DISC profiles. Read the problem exactly as written.
4:35–4:50	**Groups and Decisions—Exercise and Discussion** Give each team 15 minutes to solve the problem.
4:50–5:00	**Groups and Decisions – Discussion** Be sure to have the answer to the problem handy so you can refer to it. Remember that the purpose of the exercise is not about solving the puzzle; it's about examining and discussing the dynamics of each DISC-homogeneous group as they work to solve the puzzle. See Chapter 16 for details.

Chapter 10

Communication Origami

This workshop corresponds to Chapter 4, "Communication."

Oral communication is an essential component of teamwork. Team members are likely to choose forms of communication that suit their behavioral profiles. Someone who is a high C on the DISC profile is more likely to want to send an email than make a phone call. That person may feel less at ease when a situation warrants a conversation and will probably have to work harder than someone who is a high I. Because project teams often have several C members, there is value in helping these people increase their confidence when placed in situations that require good oral communication skills. For others, not all situations are configured to optimize productive communication. This exercise was designed to provide practice with oral communication in three different configurations and illustrate which of these configurations yields the best results.

Materials

Materials include the following:

- Origami instruction sheet
- Blank 8½ x 11-inch paper

Setup

Split the participants into three groups. This works best if each of the groups is located together. (for example, back of the room, front left side, and front right side.) Have participants pair up with someone else in their group. It's necessary to have an even number of participants so that everyone has a partner. If needed, move someone to another group to find a partner. After this, worst-case scenario, there will be one person in the room without a partner. Just have that person join one of the pairs; the exercise still works for a trio.

Designate that one person in each pair is the "guide" and the other person is the "folder." Hand out a copy of the origami instruction sheet face down to the guide and hand a blank sheet of paper to the folder. Tell the guides not to turn over the instruction sheet until told to do so.

Assign one of the following roles to each of the three groups with the following instructions:

1. **Face-to-face group:** Partners sit face to face. The guide will read the instruction sheet and communicate instructions to the folder. The guide may provide feedback to the folder but may not touch the paper being folded. The folder may not look at the instruction sheet.

2. **Side-by-side group**: Partners sit side-by-side. Both partners may look at the instruction sheet, but only the folder may touch the paper being folded.

3. **Back-to-back group**: Partners sit back to back. The guide will give instructions to the folder but may not see the paper being folded. The folder may not look at the instruction sheet.

Facilitation

Say "1-2-3-Go!" Tell the participants to create the item described on the instructions and to stand up when they finish. The exercise is straightforward and usually doesn't require any more explanation. Try to avoid any more explanation and guidance. There are unique communication dynamics that can occur within each of the three groups, and it's important to let those dynamics happen on their own.

The facilitator may want to wander and observe without offering help. You might need to remind the back-to-back partners not to look over their shoulders. Allow the exercise to continue until at least a few of the groups have successfully completed the exercise. Usually the side-by-side groups will finish first, and it's rare that a back-to-back group ever successfully completes the task.

After stopping the exercise, have one of the successful teams show off their results. It can be fun to pick on one of the back-to-back teams and illustrate how far off it was from the goal. You may even find a frustrated folder clutching onto a crumpled ball of paper!

Post-Exercise Discussion

Discuss the challenges and frustrations in each of the groups. Some key discussion points to draw out include the following:

- **Side-by-side group**
  - Ask how they worked together.
  - Discuss the challenges of the guide not being allowed to help with the folding.
  - The instructions are intentionally slightly ambiguous. Ask how they interacted to figure out instructions that were not clear.
  - Emphasis: Collaboration with full access to available resources allows people to best solve problems together.

- **Face-to-face group**
  - Ask what challenges the guide faced having to describe the instructions without being allowed to show the illustrations.
  - By seeing the work in progress, the guide adapted the instructions and injected additional information to support successful completion of the task.
  - Emphasis: Oral communication may not be enough. Written instructions and/or visual representations can be helpful to supplement the spoken word.

- **Back-to-back group**
  - By removing collaboration, visual clues, and real-time feedback, these teams were challenged, and the probability of success was low.
  - The exercise demonstrates spoken communication as it typically occurs on telephone calls, which are common to geographically dispersed teams.
  - Emphasis: The challenges faced by this group are not exclusive to spoken communication. They also occur when sending emails back and forth or when writing a requirements document and sending it to another for interpretation.

Figure 10.1 presents the instructions for the origami. (See the following page.)

Origami Instructions

1. Start with an 8½ x 11 paper.

2. Fold in half long-ways.

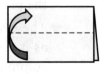

3. Fold one side in half again.

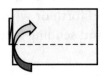

4. Flip over and fold the other side in half.

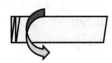

5. Unfold the side you just folded.

6. Fold in the top two corners. Include all three layers of paper.

7. Fold up the bottom two corners. Fold the bottom half back up to meet the top half. It should now look like a trapezoid.

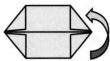

8. Fold the bottom half back up to meet the top half. It should now look like a trapezoid.

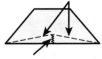

9. Make a small tear on the bottom center. Fold back a triangular shape from the corner to the center tear. Do this on both sides, then flip the trapezoid over and repeat.

10. Reach into the center of the sculpture and open.

11. Finish it off with eyes!

Figure 10.1 *Origami instructions*

Chapter 11

Bridge Building

This workshop corresponds to Chapter 3, "Team Dynamics."

Teamwork takes hard work. When a team is assigned to a new project, there are many unknown requirements, risks, and barriers that must be handled. When team members are assigned to roles, there are often predetermined expectations of the responsibilities of each of those roles. The success of the project then becomes dependent on whether all the necessary roles were assigned and that the individuals assigned to those roles have adequate skills and experience to fulfill the needs of the role.

On an agile project, there is less emphasis on prescribed roles and more emphasis on teamwork and collaboration to accomplish the work. Team members who are new to agile may come from organizations with more structure and may have a difficult time adapting to the concept of a self-organizing team. The bridge exercise was designed to help participants discover where their strengths lie as members of a team. The exercise generates a sense of urgency that encourages the members of a team to abandon preconceived notions of canned roles and instead adapt to the needs of the project and capitalize on each team member's strengths.

Materials

Materials for the workshop included the following:

- Plastic drinking straws
- Paper clips (any size)
- Cellophane tape
- Rubber bands
- Hardback textbooks
- Two tables or desks with a two-foot gap between them

Setup

Split the participants into teams of 4–6 people. Provide each team with an ample supply of drinking straws, paper clips, tape, and rubber bands. Situate the team near two desks or tables that have a two-foot gap between them. If space allows, locate the teams far enough away from each other so that they won't get in each others' way.

Facilitation

It's important for the facilitator to provide clear direction but not to provide too much information. A key learning objective of this exercise is the self-discovery process that members of each team will go through.

When all the teams are situated with their materials, provide the following instructions: "Your goal is to build a bridge between two tables using only the materials you have been provided. Your bridge should hold the weight of a textbook without collapsing. You have 20 minutes." Make note of the current time; then say, "1-2-3-Go!"

While the teams are figuring out how to start, draw a simple timeline on a whiteboard or flip chart that depicts the milestones 0, 5, 10, 15, and 20 (see Figure 11.1).

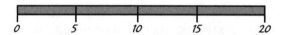

Figure 11.1 *Bridge building timeline*

Don't mention the timeline yet. Instead, casually add a twist to the requirement by stating, "Let's also see which bridge is strongest. When you finish, we'll test your bridges to see which one can hold the most books without collapsing." This casual afterthought accomplishes a couple things:

- It introduces an ambiguous goal that the team members must resolve. Together they must figure out how strong the bridge should be to beat the other teams.

- It prevents a team from creating an overly simplistic solution such as just running a couple pieces of tape between the tables and saying, "Done."

As each time milestone is reached, draw everyone's attention to the timeline and say, "Your project is 25% complete!" "...50% complete!" and so on. Update the timeline to show how much time is complete (see Figure 11.2).

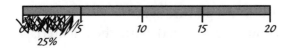

Figure 11.2 *Shaded timeline after five minutes*

Expect to see some scrambling after announcing the 75% milestone. As the clock winds down, count down the final seconds and make sure that everyone stops working when time runs out.

Although testing the bridges is not relevant to the team building point of the exercise, it does provide closure that the participants will expect. First test that each bridge can hold the weight of the textbook; then determine the winning team by piling on books (or other heavy objects) until each bridge collapses.

Post-Exercise Discussion

Several discussion points follow this exercise. The facilitator should avoid spending time focusing on specific design and engineering choices made. Rather, the discussion should center on the dynamics and behavior of the team during the exercise.

When the exercise concludes, consider some of the following discussion points:

- How long did the team dawdle before starting on the construction of bridge?

- Did a leader emerge? How long did that take, and how did the leader become the leader?

- How did the leader lead? How was it effective? How was it ineffective?

- Did someone play the role of the engineer or chief architect of the bridge?

- Who followed? Who led?

- Did anyone resist playing a follower role but resign to the role to keep the project moving forward?

- What conflict arose during the exercise? How did the team resolve that conflict?

- What changes happened to team dynamics after the project completion percent was announced?

- Did awareness that time was burning help motivate productivity, or did it detract focus?

- How did the team's behavior adapt when the non-functional requirement was introduced after the project was well underway. ("Let's also see which bridge is the strongest.")

After discussing these questions, you need to draw attention to behaviors, roles, and feelings that were exposed during the exercise. When conducting this exercise with an existing team, it's helpful to tie the learning objectives from the bridge exercise to situations that arise on an actual project the team is working on.

Chapter 12

Moon Survival

This workshop corresponds with Chapter 5, "Collaboration."

Collaboration often requires more energy than working independently. It's also likely that the total effort exerted by a team to solve a problem can greatly exceed the effort of an individual solving the problem alone. This raises the question, "Why go through the hassles of working as a group?" The Moon Survival exercise, which was developed by NASA, provides a profound demonstration of the contrast between team and individual work.

Setup

Prepare a copy of each of the following handouts for each participant:

- Moon Survival Scenario

- Moon Survival Worksheet

- Moon Survival Scoring Instructions

- Moon Survival Expert Analysis

Refer to the facilitation instructions to determine when to distribute each of these handouts. Each participant also needs a pen or pencil.

Facilitation

Start the exercise by handing out the Moon Survival Scenario sheet to each of the participants. Give them five minutes to read the sheet and ensure that everyone understands the instructions. At this point, do not discuss the scenario; just discuss the procedure for completing the individual portion of the exercise.

Individual Exercise

When everyone is ready, hand out a copy of the Moon Survival Worksheet to each participant. Give everyone 15 minutes to rank the items from most important for survival (1) to least important (15). Participants should complete the exercise independently with no discussion.

After the individual exercise, ask the participants to fold over enough of the left side of the worksheet to cover their individual rankings. This is to prevent participants from seeing each other's rankings during the team portion of the exercise.

Team Exercise

Next, organize into 4–6 person teams and have each group come up with a single ranking that the group agrees to. When the group ranking has been determined, all team members should record the group ranking on column D of their worksheets.

Scoring

Hand out a copy of the Moon Survival Scoring Instructions to each participant. When scoring has been completed, each participant should have an individual total and a team total.

This portion of the exercise may take 30–45 minutes. The facilitator plays an important role in keeping all groups on task and ensuring that they successfully agree to a ranking for the group.

Post-Exercise Discussion

Ask the participants to reveal their individual rankings to their teammates and discuss the differences. When discussing scores, remember that the lower the difference, the closer the match with the expert's ranking. Usually, the team score will be better (a lower number) than anyone on the team's individual score.

The ensuing discussion should center on why the team score beats the individual scores. Even if some individuals happen to beat the team, you should find that the team score will beat the score of the majority of its individual team members.

It's recommended that the facilitator read Chapter 5 for insight to help facilitate this discussion. Work to focus the discussion more on team dynamics than on the reasoning behind the expert choices. You are likely to find that high D participants won't be as concerned with the expert's explanation because they may not agree with it anyway. On the other hand, high C participants are unlikely to be satisfied until they are given a complete explanation for why the experts ranked the items as they did.

After you are satisfied that the participants understand the value of teamwork, you may distribute the Moon Survival Expert Analysis handout for participants to read at their leisure. As with most of the activities in this book, you might want to remind participants not to discuss the details of the exercise with others who may have an opportunity to participate in the future.

Moon Survival Scenario

Please read the scenario and wait for instructions from the facilitator.

SCENARIO

The year is 2025, and you are part of a four-member team traveling toward the Moon in the Orion spacecraft. Orion is a gum-drop-shaped spacecraft designed to carry humans from Earth to the Moon. Orion is similar in shape to but larger than the capsules used during the Apollo program. Attached, or docked, to Orion is the Lunar Surface Access Module (LSAM), which you will use to land on the Moon.

As your spacecraft enters lunar orbit, you spot the lunar outpost. This outpost has grown, having been built piece by piece during past missions. You are excited to see the outpost. It is located on a crater rim near the lunar south pole in near-constant sunlight. This location is not far from supplies of water ice that can be found in the cold, permanently shadowed part of the crater.

After transferring into the LSAM and separating from Orion, you prepare to descend to the lunar surface. Suddenly, you notice that there is a problem with the thrusters. You land safely but off course, about 80 kilometers (50 miles) from the lunar outpost. As you look across the charcoal-gray, dusty surface of the Moon, you realize your survival depends on reaching the outpost, finding a way to protect yourself until someone can reach you, or meeting a rescue party somewhere between your landing site and the outpost.

You know the Moon has basically no atmosphere or magnetosphere to protect you from space radiation. The environment is unlike any found on Earth. The regolith, or lunar soil, is a mixture of materials that includes sharp, glassy particles. The gravity field on the Moon is only one-sixth as strong as Earth's. More than 80 percent of the Moon is made up of heavily cratered highlands. Temperatures vary widely on the Moon. It can be as cold as $-193°C$ ($-315°F$) at night at its poles and as hot as $111°C$ ($232°F$) during the day at its equator.

Survival depend[s] on your mode of transportation and ability to navigate. Your basic needs for food, shelter, water, and air must be considered.

INDIVIDUAL EXERCISE

You are challenged to choose items that will help you survive. On the Moon Survival Worksheet, you will find a list of 15 items available to you. In Column A, rank these items from 1 to 15 according to their importance to you and your crew. Place the number 1 by the most important item and continue ranking the items to number 15, the least important to your survival.

STOP. Before proceeding to the next step, please fold over the left side of the Moon Survival Worksheet to hide your individual ranks; then wait for instructions from the facilitator.

Source: NASA and Jamestown Education Module EG-2006-09-25-LaRC

Individual Rank (1–15)			Moon Survival Worksheet	Team Rank (1–15)		
			Life raft A self-inflatable floatation device			
			Two 45.5-kilogram (100-pound) tanks of oxygen Pressurized tanks of oxygen			
			Space blanket A thin sheet of plastic material that is coated with a metallic reflecting layer			
			Lights with solar-powered rechargeable batteries Portable lights powered by solar batteries			
			Signal mirror A handheld mirror			
			38 liters (10 gallons) of water A container of water			
			First aid kit A basic first aid kit with pain medication and medicine for infection			
			Food concentrate Dehydrated food to which water is added			
			Magnetic compass A tool that uses a magnetic field to determine direction			
			Solar-powered radio receiver-transmitter A communication tool powered by the sun			
			Map of the Moon's surface A map showing the Moon's terrain			
			15 meters (about 50 feet) of nylon rope Manufactured rope			
			Parachute A large piece of silk cloth			
			Space suit repair kit Materials to repair tiny holes in fabric			
			Box of matches Wooden sticks with sulfur-treated heads			
Total:				Total:		

Moon Survival Scoring Instructions

B/E
12
1
9
11
10
2
5
3
14
4
6
8
13
7
15

Please follow the facilitator's instructions.

Align this page with the Moon Survival Worksheet, and enter the values on the right into the corresponding cells in both column B and column E.

For each row, calculate the value of column C by subtracting column B from column A. If less than zero, drop the negative sign (e.g., take the absolute value).

A	B	C
1	4	3
8	12	4
10	8	2

$$C = |A - B|$$
$$|1 - 4| = 3$$

Calculate the column F values using the same procedure from step 2.

Sum the total of columns C and F.

Total: 54

Compare the totals—the lower the score, the closer the match to the expert's opinion. (Golf-style scoring)

Discuss the difference between your individual score and your team score.

Moon Survival Expert Analysis

Two NASA scientists separately ranked the same items and explained their reasons for their rankings. Dr. Carlton Allen was the first expert. Dr. Allen is the curator and manager of the Astromaterials Research and Exploration Science (ARES) Astromaterials Acquisition and Curation Office. This office is responsible for protecting, preserving, and distributing extraterrestrial samples to help others learn more about solar system exploration. These samples include the Apollo Moon rocks and regoliths, Antarctic meteorites, and particles of solar wind. Dr. Allen's background is in planetary science. The second expert was John Gruener, who is a flight systems engineer at NASA's Johnson Space Center, and his background is in aerospace engineering and physical sciences with an emphasis in planetary geology. He has worked as a rocket scientist designing missions to the Moon and Mars, as a space farmer growing plants in advanced life-support systems and as a planetary scientist studying the rocks and soils on Mars.

Both experts agreed that the type of lander in which you were traveling would determine your course of action if you landed on the wrong place on the Moon. If you were in a two-stage lander (one stage for descent and one stage for ascent, like the Apollo lunar module), they suggested that you terminate the surface mission, head back to orbit, rendezvous with Orion in lunar orbit, and head home.

If returning home were not a choice and you were stuck on the Moon, the experts suggested that you sit tight and wait for someone at the outpost to come and get you. They agreed that the safest thing to do in this situation, as in most emergencies, is to stay put and call for help.

If someone from the outpost cannot reach you, the experts felt that you had no option other than to try to make it to the outpost. The rankings and explanations in Table 12.1 indicate how each expert ranked the items to help you reach the outpost.

Table 12.1 *Expert Analysis*

Rank	Item	Explanation for Expert's Rank
1	Two 45.5-kilogram (100-pound) tanks of oxygen Pressurized tanks of oxygen	Expert 1: "With basically no atmosphere on the Moon, oxygen (O2) to breathe is the most pressing survival need. The average person needs about 0.84 kilograms (a little less than 2 pounds) of O2 per day." Expert 2: "Oxygen to breathe is the most important survival need, since the Moon has virtually no atmosphere."
2	38 liters (10 gallons) of water A container of water	Expert 1: "Though we believe there is some water in the form of ice on the Moon, there is no liquid water. Water is essential to all life. Currently, each astronaut aboard the International Space Station (ISS) uses about 11 liters (3 gallons) of water daily." Expert 2: "Water is another basic survival need for the astronauts. Because there is no liquid water on the Moon, the astronauts will need the water they brought with them to survive."
3	Food concentrate Dehydrated food to which water is added	Expert 1: "Food concentrate is a good source of food and an efficient way to carry it." Expert 2: "Although the food concentrate must have water added to be useful, it is lightweight and easy to carry, meeting a third basic need for survival."

Rank	Item	Explanation for Expert's Rank
4	**Solar-powered radio receiver-transmitter** A communication tool powered by the sun	Expert 1: "Hopefully people from the lunar outpost are looking for you while you are trying to reach them. A solar- powered radio receiver-transmitter is important to maintain this communication." Expert 2: "As people from the lunar outpost are looking for you, you should try to reach them. Main-taining communication with your outpost is essential."
5	**First aid kit** A basic first aid kit with pain medication and medicine for infec-tion	Expert 1: "No matter where you are, a first aid kit is a good idea. Be sure you carry pain medication and medicine for infections." Expert 2: "A first aid kit takes up little space and may be important to have in case of illness or injury."
6	**Map of the Moon's surface** A map showing the Moon's terrain	Expert 1: "A map of the Moon's surface is your primary way to identify your location and to help you navigate." Expert 2: "With no other direc-tional tools available, a map of the Moon's surface is the most impor-tant means of finding your way from one location to another."
7	**Space suit repair kit** Materials to repair tiny holes in fabric	Expert 1: "You cannot afford to have any tears in your space suit. Your suit protects you from harsh conditions while you make your way to the lunar outpost. The soil of the Moon (regolith) 'sticks' to space suits and equipment. It is very sharp, like tiny fragments of glass or coral, and can cut holes that put your life at risk." Expert 2: "Your space suit protects you from the harsh conditions on the Moon. The sharp soil of the Moon can cut tiny holes in the suit, which may compromise its effective-ness."

Rank	Item	Explanation for Expert's Rank
8	**15 meters (about 50 feet) of nylon rope** Manufactured rope	Expert 1: "The nylon rope is useful in scaling cliffs or craters you may have to cross. To prevent injury or in case you cannot walk, rope is helpful for tying you to others." Expert 2: "The rope makes dragging the life raft easier or may come in handy when crossing difficult terrain."
9	**Space blanket** A thin sheet of plastic material that is coated with a metallic reflecting layer	Expert 1: "The space blanket helps reduce heat loss from a person's body. The reflective material reflects about 80 percent of the wearer's body heat back to the body. The reflected side is also used to prevent absorption of sunlight." Expert 2: "The space blanket is used to insulate the oxygen and water from the hot daytime temperatures. Temperatures vary widely on the Moon. It can be as cold as -193°C (-315°F) at night at its poles and as hot as 111°C (232°F) during the day at its equator."
10	**Signal mirror** A handheld mirror	Expert 1: "The signal mirror is an important way to communicate during the daylight. The Moon's daylight is brighter and harsher than Earth's. There is virtually no atmosphere to scatter the light, no clouds to shade it, and no ozone layer to block the sun burning ultraviolet light." Expert 2: "The signal mirror is used as a form of communication if the radio is not working."

Rank	Item	Explanation for Expert's Rank
11	**Lights with solar-powered rechargeable batteries** Portable lights powered by solar batteries	Expert 1: "These lights allow for nighttime travel. The nights on the Moon are brighter than nights on Earth, at least on the side of the Moon that is facing Earth. With its clouds and oceans, Earth reflects more light than the dark Moon rocks. Earthlight on the Moon is much brighter than moonlight on Earth." Expert 2: "The lights are helpful if you travel across large shadowed areas. Some areas in the polar regions are permanently dark."
12	**Life raft** A self-inflatable floatation device	Expert 1: "The life raft makes a great sled for carrying the oxygen and water." Expert 2: "A life raft is of little use for survival on the Moon. Although it could be used to drag heavy items, the sharp regolith would quickly puncture the raft."
13	**Parachute** A large piece of silk cloth	Expert 1: "Compared to other items, this item is of little use." Expert 2: "Parachute silk comes in handy as a backup sled to the life raft, or as shade."
14	**Magnetic compass** A tool that uses a magnetic field to determine direction	Expert 1: "The Moon has no global magnetic field, which makes a magnetic compass virtually useless." Expert 2: "The compass is virtually useless because there is no Moon-wide magnetic field."
15	**Box of matches** Wooden sticks with sulfur-treated heads	Expert 1: "Matches are virtually useless on the Moon because there is little oxygen." Expert 2: "With little oxygen on the Moon, the matches are useless."

Chapter 13

BalderDISC

This workshop corresponds with Chapter 6, "Behavior and Teams."

The "wheel" (as described in Chapter 6) is an excellent tool for enhancing team communication on an agile project because the entire team can quickly and easily see who will naturally get along and who may conflict. Additionally, DISC reports are highly valuable because they contain a lot of detail about each individual. Many DISC reports include a comprehensive section that describes numerous characteristics of the individual, how best to communicate with the individual, and more.

DISC is highly accurate but should not be considered an exact science. Moreover, the reports can be lengthy. Therefore, creating a communication chart that summarizes each team member's most appropriate characteristics and communication styles can be useful for each team member:

- To see the components of the report that individuals believe best depict who they are.

- To know how to most effectively communicate with each individual.

It is worth the time it takes for all members on an agile team to understand one another at a level deep enough to comprehend what makes them tick and how they will behave. This can enhance communication effectiveness and can often avoid conflicts that would have arisen during the project if the team had not gone through this exercise. Human conflict can be more costly to a project than defects in code.

Materials

Materials for this exercise include the following:

- Highlighter

- Index cards

- A set of cards you create for each player containing five voting cards that have the numbers 1, 2, 3, 4, and 5 (one number per card)

- Computer, spreadsheet (or word processor), and printer

- Detailed DISC report for each participant

Setup

Prior to starting this exercise, have every member of the team take a DISC assessment from a provider that provides a detailed DISC report describing the individual as well as a wheel. The free DISC provided in this book provides only a DISC graph. To perform this exercise, you must find a DISC provider (by searching the Internet) and request all participants take the DISC assessment and bring a printed report to the workshop.

During the workshop, all individuals review each section of their own reports and highlight the sentences that they believe most accurately reflect who they are and how best to communicate with them. This can be as much or as little of the report they feel is important for other team members to know what makes them tick and who they are.

Have each individual select the top four sentences they feel best depict who they are and are most important to share with the team. Next each individual should create one sentence that is not a true statement of who they are. They can either make up a lie or could take one of the statements in their report and say the opposite. For example, if the report indicates, "Flattery will always generate a positive reaction with him." You might choose to say the opposite, "Do not try to use flattery to try to persuade him." Write all four sentences on an index card (in any random order)—see Figure 13.1 for an example.

Earl

1. He has an extremely high trust level and is optimistic.
2. He likes to develop people and build organizations.
3. He believes rules exist to serve rather than to be followed by him.
4. (Lie) Do not try and use flattery to try and persuade him.
5. He has the ability to look at the whole problem; for example, thinking about relationships, being concerned about the feeling of others, and focusing on the real impact of his decisions and actions.

Figure 13.1 *Example index card*

Facilitation

Each person takes a turn by reading his or her cards containing five sentences (four truths about themselves and one lie). After someone reads a card, everyone else in the room votes by holding up a voting card containing the number they feel is the lie. The facilitator should say, "One, two, three, vote" for everyone in the room to hold up their guess at the same time to prevent unfairness.

Each player that guesses the correct lie scores one point. In the preceding example, every player holding up the number "4" would win one point. If no one in the room guesses the correct lie, the card reader gets two points. In the preceding example, if no one guessed a "4," the reader would score two points. At the end of each round, have the reader tell the team his or her dominant DISC profile element. For example, Earl might say, "I am an "I."" Whoever has the most points after everyone has taken a turn reading wins the game.

This is a fun exercise that enables the team members to bond and get to know one another at a personal level.

Post-Exercise Discussion

This exercise can enable the team to more quickly move along the forming, storming, norming, performing stages as mentioned in Chapter 3, "Team Dynamics." It can also help avoid conflicts that would occur without having a better understanding of each of the team members' behavioral tendencies.

Allow open discussion to occur during the facilitation by the team members.

In the post-discussion, ask the team to quickly reassemble the room into four quadrants by the highest element of each individual's DISC profiles—that is, have all the D's sit in one section of the room, all the C's in another, and so on. Point out the importance of the quadrants. That is, there will be natural conflicts that occur between the groups. D's and C's, for example, will conflict because the C's might appear to the D's to be overly quiet and take too long to ponder the details, whereas the D's might appear to the C's to be outspokenly rude and always want to skip the details and drive to a solution. Emphasize the importance of embracing the DISC to better accept others and understand why they behave the way they do. Encourage people to use the language of DISC in situations in which they feel conflicts are starting to arise.

Reinforce that the best teams comprise a blend of behavioral profiles. You want team members to consist of a combination of D's, who will make quicker decisions and help drive the project; C's, who will focus on the details as they analyze requirements, test, and write code; S's, who will bring harmony to the team; and I's, who will keep the communication going, optimism high, and energy flowing. It is healthy to have some team members optimistically viewing the project in a glass-is-half-full perspective, whereas others are continually concerned about the project's status or level of quality. Therefore the best teams have a mix of behavioral profiles, which in turn tends to also result in natural conflict.

After the workshop is complete, it is recommended that the facilitator create a Team Communication Chart containing each team member's highlighted sentences. This chart should not be limited to the four top elements that individuals selected to place on their index cards. This chart could be created in a spreadsheet or in a word processor. Either email the chart to all members of the team or post it on a wall in the project room.

Additionally, the team should create a team wheel. As an example, Figure 13.2 shows a team wheel if the team chose The Abelson Group as their DISC provider. Have all team members write their names or initials on the wheel corresponding to their adaptive/work behavior provided in their report. If any team member's natural behavior is extremely different than their adaptive behavior, have them write their name or initials in a different color.

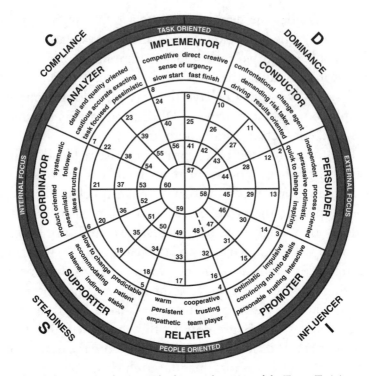

The Abelson DISC Behaviors Wheel is an adaptation of the Target Training International, LTD. Wheel and is a trademark of The Abelson Group™

Figure 13.2 *Example Team Wheel template*

Chapter 14

Assessing Concordance and Discordance

This workshop corresponds with Chapter 5, "Collaboration."

It's helpful to know how easily the members of a team are influenced by the rest of the membership. When a leader knows if a team has more conformant versus discordant tendencies, it's easier to determine how closely a team's decision-making behavior must be managed. When the results of this exercise are shared and discussed with a team, the team may be more open to improving the efficiency of discussing topics and making decisions.

Materials

Materials include the following:

- Weight Plot Chart
- Three blank slips of paper per person

Setup

The most important element of this exercise is a prepared facilitator who has the confidence and willingness to expose his/her weight to the group. A different measurable attribute could be used, but body weight tends to work well.

Start by handing out three blank slips of paper to each participant and make sure that everyone has something to write with. Prepare the blank weight plot so that it may be revealed with plotted data during each of the three rounds of the exercise. This could be done on a white board, on a spreadsheet, or simply plotted on a piece of paper that is passed around the room. Figure 14.3 contains a blank weight plot template.

Facilitation

Start by asking everyone in the room to guess your weight. Have them write down that guess on one of the slips of paper without discussion or collaboration. Gather up everyone's guesses and plot them along the first column of the weight plot. Be sure to plot the guesses along a straight vertical line (see Figure 14.1). When plotting two guesses with the same value, go ahead and offset the plots a bit to depict that there is more than one guess for that value.

When plotting the guesses, do not reveal who made each guess. After all the guesses have been plotted, reveal the chart to the group and ask everyone to make another guess. Do this without further explanation or instruction. Plot the results, reveal the results, and repeat for a third round.

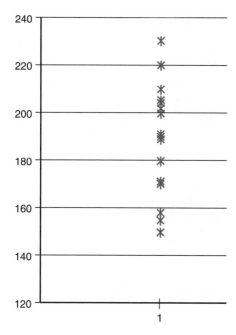

Figure 14.1 *Weight guessing plot (Round 1)*

After finishing three rounds, assess the graph and discuss the results with the group.

Post-Exercise Discussion

The goal of this exercise is to understand the conformance/discordance level of the group. The shape of the plot created in this exercises reveals this. The facilitator starts by showing the plot and explaining the group's behavior that it reveals.

The depictions of plotted data presented in Figure 14.2 show two contrasting possible outcomes: On the left is a group with a high level of conformance and a low level of discordance. The plot on the right depicts low (or no) conformance and high discordance. The facilitator may

choose to draw these shapes and discuss the different behavior characteristics of each of the groups that each of
these shapes represents. It could be interesting to ask how
individuals would feel if they were a member of each of
these groups; then contrast those feelings with the actual
group plot from the exercise. This discussion can expose
opportunities for improving the dynamics of the group.

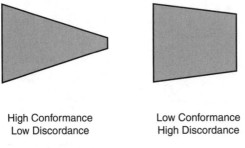

High Conformance   Low Conformance
Low Discordance   High Discordance

Figure 14.2 *Data plots*

After reading Chapter 5, you may now realize that the
point of this exercise is not to grade the group as positive
or negative. Rather, the point is to better understand the
magnitude of influence members of the group have on one
another. When discussing the conformance profile of the
group, accept the behavioral tendencies of the group and
focus the conversation on how to operate most productively because of (or despite) what the profile indicates.

Figure 14.3 *Weight plot chart template*

Chapter 15

Change Exercise

This workshop corresponds with Chapter 7, "Change."

Change can be difficult for some people to talk about or to even think about. Addressing need for change head-on can be fruitful and is an essential prerequisite to making change happen. This exercise is designed to soften the severity of discussions about change through the use of a fun and lively game. The fast-paced nature of the exercise avoids arduous emotionally charged discussions about change. Rather, it facilitates quick brainstorming about things that need to be changed without stewing over the challenges or consequences—almost like pulling off a bandage in one quick swipe.

Overview

The room is split into small groups that will be competing against each other. Each team will sit in front of a flip chart or white board while one member of each team is drawing a picture of a desired change. The facilitator shows a card containing a description of a desired change on it to the designated drawer on each team. Each team should guess what is being drawn by shouting out the answer. Drawing responsibility rotates on each team so that everyone serves as drawer and guesser. The first team to guess correctly earns a point. At the end of the game, the team with the most points wins.

Setup

The materials required are simple:

- Blank 3x5 cards

- Pens

Prior to beginning the game, hand out stacks of 3x5 cards and ask all participants to grab a card and draw a vertical line down the middle of it, dividing it into two sections. Label the left side "Now" and the right side "Goal" (see Figure 15.1). Next, on the left half of the card, write a phrase or a single sentence describing something that is undesirable now. On the right side, write a phrase or single sentence describing a corresponding positive goal. When writing the goal, consider the changes that will need to occur in order to attain the stated goal. Give five minutes to fill out as many cards as possible. Ask the participants to work individually and not share or discuss the information on their cards. Tell them that others will be reading their cards, so be helpful by writing or printing as neatly as possible. Have the participants write their names on the back of their index cards.

Collect all the cards and mix them up for use during the next part of the exercise.

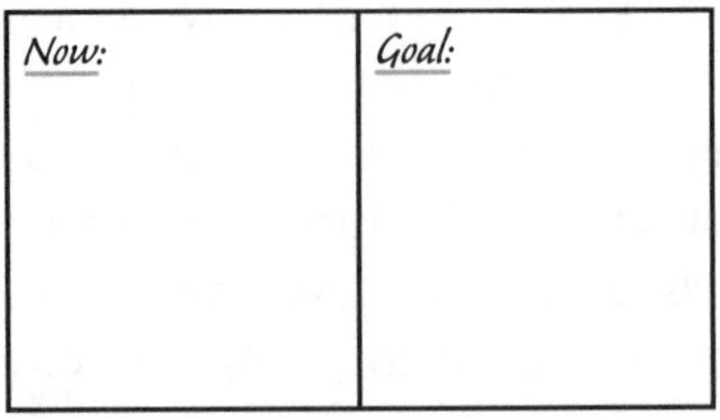

Now:	Goal:

Figure 15.1 *The card should look like this.*

Examples include the following:

Now: The project requires skills we don't have on the team.

Goal: Training is provided for everyone needing new skills.

Now: Each team member is expected to juggle multiple projects at once.

Goal: 100% dedicated resources on the project.

Now: Daily standup meetings take too long.

Goal: Everyone follows the Scrum meeting format in the daily meetings.

The Drawing Board

Decide how many teams will compete and designate a space for each team to work. Remember that the facilitator will observe all the teams during the game to listen for a winning answer, so try to position the teams where the facilitator can see and hear each team. The overlapping chaos contributes to the high-energy fun of this game. Because all teams are solving the same "puzzle" simultaneously, some individuals may eavesdrop on what the other teams are doing. In the spirit of the purpose of the game (open communication) there's no need to be concerned when this happens.

The Teams

Divide up the room with approximately the same number of people on each team. There are no specialized skills required for this game, so there's no benefit in trying to "even up" the teams in any manner other than head count. If the teams don't have the same number of people, it will not affect the outcome of the game. The goal is to ensure that everyone has a chance to participate as a drawer and as a guesser.

Facilitation

For each round, the facilitator picks a card off the pile and reads the name on the back of the card. This person comes up to the front of the room and helps the facilitator monitor this round.

Have each team select one person to be the drawer for the round. Make sure the drawer has a pen and is standing in front of the drawing board before the game begins.

Give the following instructions to all participants:

"Shortly I will be showing one of the change cards to each of the drawers. When I say 'Go!' the drawer should draw the desired change. After you read the card, focus on the section labeled 'Goal' and draw a picture representing that change. You may not use words, letters, or numbers, and you may not speak while drawing."

Typically, most participants are not going to be skilled artists. If any of the players happen to have artistic talent, the game moves so fast that there is little time to create a masterpiece. Master doodlers, on the other hand, may find the game easier than others. Some things are easier to draw than others, and lack of artistic talent can generate a lot of laughter!

For example, when reading a card containing the goal, "Training is provided for everyone needing new skills," one drawer might try to show some depiction of a classroom or a teacher. Another might draw a metaphor or even a homonym (such as picture of a train).

"As you draw, your teammates will try to guess the change that you are drawing. Listen closely to the guesses, and when you hear the correct answer, point to the person who made the guess. The facilitator will ask the player to repeat the answer and judge whether it is correct. If the answer is correct, it scores a point for that team, and the round is over."

Because of the possible complexity of each described change, it's rare that anyone's guess precisely matches what's on the card. The person who wrote the original card will judge whether a team's guess is close enough to count as correct.

When someone makes a correct guess, a point is earned for that team, and the round ends. The facilitator should determine how to end the game. Often, a time limit or a specified number of rounds is used. When the end of the game has been reached, the team with the most points wins!

Post-Exercise Discussion

After the game concludes, it's important to have a discussion about the change goals. The facilitator should be prepared to delicately handle changes that cause discomfort for some. Additionally, there may be disagreements that require some mediation.

A structured way to facilitate the post-game discussion is to use the S-T-O-W technique. On a white board or flip chart, draw a target with four rings. Mark the center "S"; then mark each subsequent ring with "T," "O," and "W." Write a legend next to the target showing Self, Team, Organization, and World (see Figure 15.2). This target will be used to specify the subject of each change.

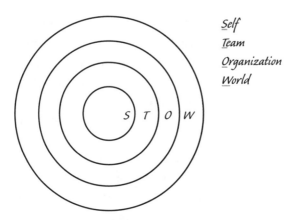

Self
Team
Organization
World

Figure 15.2 *The target*

Next, retrieve the first change card from the game. Write "1." followed by the change goal from the card. Ask the participants where this change belongs in the target and write the number in the corresponding ring on the target.

For example, some may feel that "100% dedicated resources assigned to the project" may fall in the "Team" ring, whereas others believe it belongs in the "Organization" ring. This offers an opportunity to discuss where and who can make this change happen. You might discuss that if the team is not empowered to change how individuals are assigned to projects, the change should likely be escalated to the organization level. This approach can center the discussion on how to get to decision makers in the organization that have the authority to make the change happen.

During discussions about changes to the organization, be prepared for statements such as "It'll never change; it's been that way forever," or "Nobody knows why we do things this way; we just do." Recently, in a presentation about agile software development to 100 executives at a major corporation, one of the executives interrupted the presentation with the comment, "This agile stuff makes sense, but it will never work here. Our organization would never permit such a radical change to the way we run projects." Another executive in the room piped in, "What are you talking about? We are the organization. We are the reason we do things the way we do. If we are ever going to change, it has to start here, with us." It's funny how many people can refer to an organization as an abstraction, as though they are not the organization. Recognition of the presence of individuals in an organization who wield decision-making ability is an important step in accommodating changes in organizations.

For change items assigned to the "Self" ring, the discussion will be quite different—centered on how to encourage individuals on the team to change. Be cautious during these discussions. Talking about how to change an abstraction (the organization) or change other individuals is vastly different than discussing changes to one's self. Also be cautious to avoid directed criticism. If John says, "Mary needs to avoid discussing irrelevant details during the standup meeting," Mary may feel cornered, vulnerable, and uncomfortable. Try generalizing "self" changes so that they could potentially apply to any or all individuals on the team.

On an agile team, changes to "Team" offer a great opportunity that could be resolved during the exercise. The lightweight organizational structure of a team on an agile project provides the leverage needed to efficiently introduce change. If the team decides to change the way standup meetings are held or how work is assigned, it shouldn't require any bureaucracy. It ought to make a decision together and move forward.

Changes to "World" may seem unnecessary because it's beyond the power of a group to change the world. However, identification and discussion of items that influence us and that we cannot change can be helpful. Working around (and despite) immutable things is a necessary element of how a healthy team works productively together.

Chapter 16

Groups and Decisions

This workshop corresponds with Chapter 5, "Collaboration." It enables your team to better understand group dynamics and decisions.

Setup

For a group whose members have all completed the DISC assessment, organize into DISC-homogeneous teams. Create separate teams, combining the D's, I's, S's, and C's into separate teams based on the element of their profiles that are the most dominant (highest point in the DISC graph).

Give the following problem to each team and examine the unique dynamics of each group as they work to come up with a solution.

When reading the problem to the groups, it's important to read it just as it is written. This ensures that the problem is described clearly and unambiguously to everyone. Also the final instruction, which asks for the optimal solution, can have an impact on the dynamics of each of the groups when solving the problem.

The Problem

A farmer needs to transport a goose, a fox, and a sack of grain across a river. His boat is so small that there is only room for himself and one of the others at a time.

If he leaves the fox and goose together, the fox will kill the goose. If he leaves the goose and the grain together, the goose will eat the grain.

What is the optimal solution for getting the farmer, the goose, the fox, and the grain all to the other side of the river?

If you have a group of high C's, for example, they may solve the puzzle yet strain their brains to find a better solution. A group of D's, on the other hand, may strive to solve the problem faster than the other groups. (Even though speed was never expressed as a measurement of success.)

The Solution

The default solution to this age-old puzzle is as follows:

- The farmer crosses with the goose, leaving the fox and the grain.

- Farmer returns, leaving goose on the other side.

- Farmer crosses with the fox.

- Farmer leaves the fox and returns with the goose.

- Farmer leaves the goose and crosses with the grain.

- Farmer leaves the fox and the grain, crosses back and returns with the goose.

Bear in mind that the purpose of the exercise is not about solving the puzzle; it's about examining the dynamics of each DISC-homogeneous group as they work to solve the puzzle.

It's possible that some clever team members may introduce solutions that others may believe are "against the rules." For example, "Geese can swim, so he keeps the goose tied to the boat as he crosses with the fox; then returns for the grain" or "The farmer puts the fox and the grain in the boat, and swims with the goose along-side the boat." These revelations may be moments of brilliance to some and may be considered cheating by others.

Again, focus on the behavioral dynamics of each group and focus the discussions on why they interacted the way they did and how important it is to maintain awareness of those behavioral tendencies when functioning as a member of a project team.

DISC-Homogeneous Behavior

During the previous group exercise, following are some of the observations you might make:

- **D Predominant Group**: Most competitive; trying to work quickly to solve the problem the fastest; loudest; multiple people speaking, interrupting one another; very happy if they "win."

- **I Predominant Group**: Laughing and having fun; encouraging one another; straying off topic; remaining positive and optimistic.

- **S Predominant Group**: Relatively quiet and calm; supportive of one another; coming up with the solution as a team; less concerned with speed or winning.

- **C Predominant Group**: Overanalyzing the problem; relatively quiet; taking a systematic and academic approach to solving the problem.

If you try the exercise with a mixture of behavioral profiles, some are likely to be influenced by others, whereas others are unlikely to be easily influenced. For example, the D's and I's will tend to dominate the conversation over the S's and C's.

Note that it's possible that one or more participants may know the solution to the puzzle because they've seen it before. When this occurs, it doesn't necessarily spoil the exercise. It might be interesting to see a D work to convince the other D's that his/her answer is correct—or to see an S not reveal knowing the answer already in order to allow the others to experience the enjoyment of solving the puzzle. The key to successfully facilitating this exercise is to observe all group dynamics keenly and to discuss those observations when the puzzle-solving portion of the exercise is complete.

Appendix

How to Take the DISC

This appendix provides a free DISC assessment. In each row in the DISC Assessment, select the word that describes you most. Color in that shape under the M column with a pen/pencil. Of the remaining three words, pick the word that describes you least and color in that shape with a pen/pencil under the L column. Picture yourself in a work environment. Do not over analyze. You should select whichever word comes to mind as your gut reaction. It should take approximately 15–20 minutes to complete all 26 rows.

For example, in the first row of words, assume you believe that "daring" describes you most and "accurate" describes you least, you would color in the shapes as shown in Figure A.1.

Figure A.1 *Example taking DISC Assessment*

Please note that this instrument works only if your input is a reflection of who you are. That is, do not try and select who you "want" to be. Picture yourself at work and be honest with who you are. Remember, there are no right or wrong answers and no good or bad behavioral profiles.

The best teams contain a blend of all profiles. So begin filling in your assessment (see Figure A.2).

	M	L		M	L		M	L		M	L
accurate	◠	◠	daring	▽	□	good-humored	▽	○	even-tempered	☆	☆
adventurous	□	□	dedicated	☆	▽	follower	▽	◠	charismatic	○	○
refined	▽	◠	powerful	□	□	sociable	○	○	tolerant	☆	☆
influential	○	▽	unassuming	◠	◠	gentle	☆	☆	innovative	▽	□
outgoing	○	○	easily intimidated	☆	☆	aggressive	□	▽	apprehensive	▽	◠
open minded	◠	▽	welcoming	▽	○	bold	□	□	sensible	☆	☆
cooperative	◠	◠	persistent	□	□	attracts people	○	○	sweet	▽	☆
driver	□	□	analyzer	◠	◠	team player	☆	☆	influencer	○	○
supportive	☆	☆	strong-willed	▽	□	amenable	◠	▽	cheerful	○	○
motivational	○	▽	obedient	▽	☆	fearless	□	▽	introverted, shy	▽	◠
thoughtful	☆	▽	submissive	▽	◠	admirable	○	▽	assertive	□	□
precise	◠	▽	candid	□	□	even keeled	▽	☆	jovial	○	○
giving	☆	☆	dynamic	▽	○	disciplined	◠	▽	determined	□	□
considerate	☆	☆	joyful	▽	○	competitive	□	□	agrees with others	▽	◠
determined	□	▽	persuasive	○	○	cautious	◠	◠	pleasant	☆	▽
compliant	☆	▽	unbeatable	□	□	picky	▽	◠	fun	○	○
gutsy	□	□	tactful	◠	▽	articulate	▽	○	content	☆	☆
leader	□	□	mentor	○	○	doer	◠	◠	harmonizer	☆	☆
tolerates others	☆	☆	self-sufficient	□	□	sociable	○	○	quiet	◠	▽
hospitable	☆	☆	popular	○	○	restless	□	□	organized	◠	◠
pioneering	□	□	optimistic	○	○	respectful	◠	▽	obliging	☆	☆
reserved	☆	☆	conservative	▽	◠	conversational	○	○	decision-maker	□	□
impatient	▽	▽	agreeable	◠	◠	cooperative	☆	▽	energetic	▽	□
full of compassion	▽	☆	tolerant	▽	◠	self-assured	○	▽	forceful	□	□
flexible	◠	▽	casual	▽	☆	confrontational	□	□	light hearted	○	○
at ease	▽	☆	confident	□	□	trusting	☆	○	peaceful	◠	◠

Figure A.2 *DISC Assessment*

Next, add up the colored-in shapes in the four M columns and place the totals in Figure A.3. (The total of all the numbers should equal 26.)

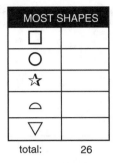

Figure A.3 *Template to enter Most values*

Now add up the colored-in shapes in the four L columns and place the totals in Figure A.4. (The total of all the numbers should equal 26.)

Figure A.4 *Template to enter Least values*

Now you are ready to plot your data. Plot the shapes, using the template in Figure A.7, by coloring in the graph up to the number of each shape. For example, if the number of Ds in the Most columns add up to 15, take your pencil or highlighter and color in the squares from the bottom to top until you reach the number 15. Not all numbers are listed in the graph, so color to the closest number (or between the two numbers that are closest to yours). Do this for both the Most and Least graphs. For example, assume your values are as shown in Figure A.5.

MOST SHAPES		
□	D	15
○	I	7
☆	S	1
◠	C	2
▽	-	1
		26

LEAST SHAPES		
□	D	1
○	I	3
☆	S	9
◠	C	10
▽	-	3
		26

Figure A.5 *Example of DISC results adding up values*

These values would result in the graphs shown in Figure A.6 for the Adapted (Most) and Natural (Least) behaviors. An individual's dominant behaviors are depicted by the elements above the bolded midline. In these graphs, the individual's behavioral profile would be a DI.

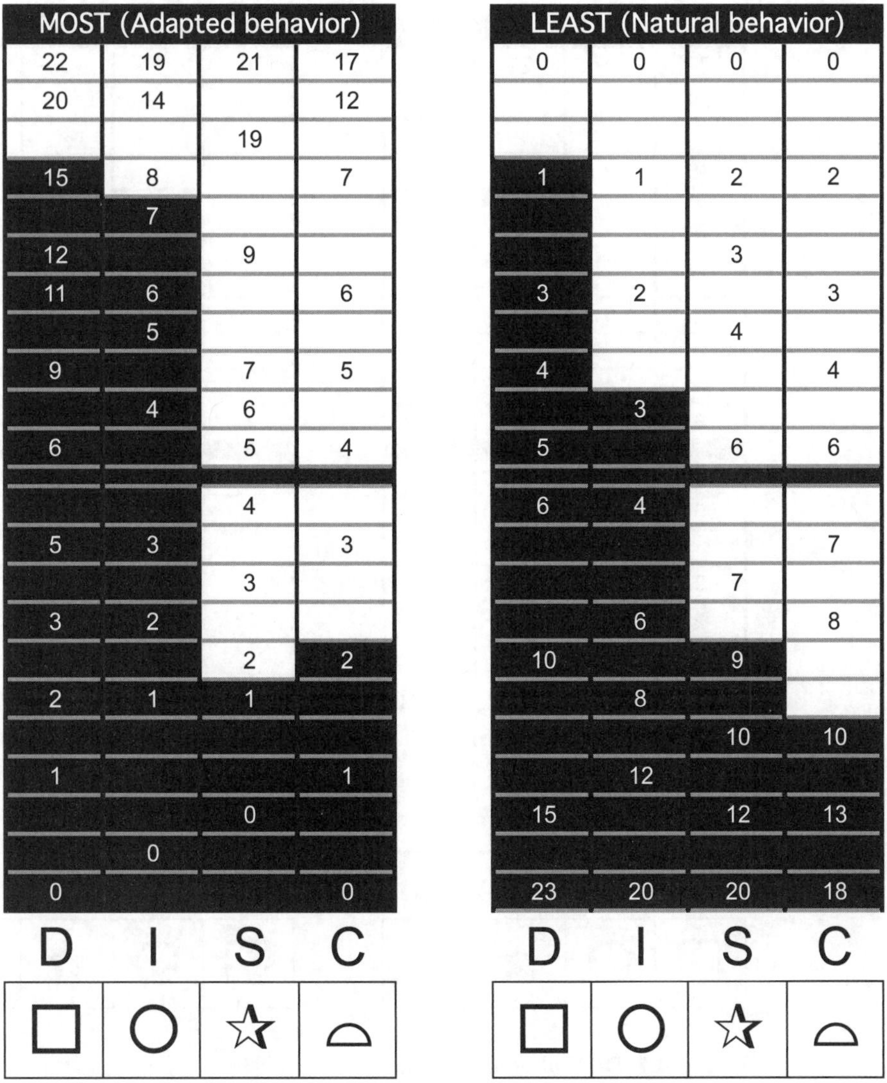

MOST (Adapted behavior)

D	I	S	C
22	19	21	17
20	14		12
		19	
15	8		7
	7		
12		9	
11	6		6
	5		
9		7	5
	4	6	
6		5	4
		4	
5	3		3
		3	
3	2		
		2	2
2	1	1	
1			1
		0	
	0		
0			0

LEAST (Natural behavior)

D	I	S	C
0	0	0	0
1	1	2	2
		3	
3	2		3
		4	
4			4
	3		
5		6	6
6	4		
			7
		7	
	6		8
10		9	
	8		
		10	10
	12		
15		12	13
23	20	20	18

D   I   S   C

Figure A.6 *Example of DISC plotting results*

The template in Figure A.7 should be used to plot your results.

MOST (Adapted behavior)			
22	19	21	17
20	14		12
		19	
15	8		7
	7		
12		9	
11	6		6
	5		
9		7	5
	4	6	
6		5	4
		4	
5	3		3
		3	
3	2		
		2	2
2	1	1	
1			1
		0	
	0		
0			0
D	**I**	**S**	**C**
□	○	☆	◠

LEAST (Natural behavior)			
0	0	0	0
1	1	2	2
		3	
3	2		3
		4	
4			4
	3		
5		6	6
6	4		
			7
		7	
	6		8
10		9	
	8		
		10	10
	12		
15		12	13
23	20	20	18
D	**I**	**S**	**C**
□	○	☆	◠

Figure A.7 *DISC plotting template*

Note that the preceding exercise yields a simple DISC graph for you to depict your dominant behavioral profile. See Chapter 2, "Behavior and Individuals," for details describing the DISC behavioral profiles, and see Chapter 6, "Behavior and Teams," for an explanation of adaptive and natural behaviors. We advise that you take a full DISC assessment from a provider that analyzes and provides additional information using all behavioral elements and not one that simply provides a DISC graph. In addition to the graphs, the results should include detailed text describing numerous characteristics of the individual, how best to communicate or not to communicate with the individual, and a "wheel" (as described in Chapter 6). You can find many DISC providers by simply searching in your favorite browser.

References

"A Theory of Human Motivation," *Psychological Review* 50(4) (1943): 370–96.

Beck, Kent and Mike Beedle, et al., www.agilemanifesto. org., 2001.

Buckingham, Marcus, and Donald O. Clifton. *Now, Discover Your Strengths*. New York: Free Press, 2001.

Cockburn, Alistair. *Agile Software Development*. Boston: Addison-Wesley, 2002.

Galton, Francis, "One Vote, One Value," *Nature*, 1907.

Galton, "Vox Populi," *Nature*, 1907.

Gilbreth, Frank B. and Ernestine Gilbreth Carey. *Cheaper by the Dozen*. New York: T.Y. Crowell Co., 1948.

Golding, William. *Lord of the Flies*. New York: Coward-McCann, 1962.

Hammer, Michael (1990), "Reengineering Work: Don't Automate, Obliterate," *Harvard Business Review*, Jul/Aug 1990, 104–112.

Exploration: Then and Now—Survival! Lesson at http:// www.nasa.gov/audience/foreducators/topnav/materials/ listbytype/Survival_Lesson.html.

Landsberger, Henry A. *Hawthorne Revisited, Management and the Worker: Its Critics, and Developments in Human Relations in Industry.* Ithaca, N.Y.: Cornell University, 1958.

Marston, William Moulton. *Emotions of Normal People.* London: K. Paul, Trench, Trubner & Co. Ltd.; 1928.

McGregor, Douglas, and Joel Gershenfeld. *The human Side of Enterprise.* Annotated ed. New York: McGraw-Hill, 2006.

Maslow, A.H. *Motivation and Personality*, Third Edition, Harper and Row Publishers, 1987.

Schwaber, K. "Scrum Development Process," in OOPSLA Business Object Design and Implementation Workshop, J. Sutherland, et al., Editors. Springer: London, 1997.

Senge, Peter M. *The Fifth Discipline: The Art and Practice of the Learning Organization.* New York: Doubleday/ Currency, 1990.

Spranger, Eduard, and Paul John William Pigors. *Types of men: The Psychology and Ethics of Personality.* Halle (Saale): M. Niemeyer, 1928.

Stacey, Ralph. *Strategic Management and Organisational Dynamics*, Second Edition. Prentice Hall, 2007.

Surowiecki, James. *The Wisdom of Crowds: Why the Many Are Smarter Than The Few.* London: Abacus, 2005.

Takeuchi, Hirotaka, and Nonaka, Ikujiro. "The New New Product Development Game." *Harvard Business Review,* January–February 1986.

Taylor, Frederick W. *Scientific Management: Comprising Shop Management, the Principles of Scientific Management, Testimony Before the Special House Committee.* New York: Harper, 1911.

Treynor, Jack L. "Market Efficiency and the Bean Jar Experiment," *Financial Analysts Journal*, May/June 1987, Vol. 43, No. 3: 50–53.

Tuckman, Bruce (1965). "Developmental Sequence in Small Groups." *Psychological Bulletin* 63(6): 384–99. Reprinted with permission in Group Facilitation, Spring 2001.

Index

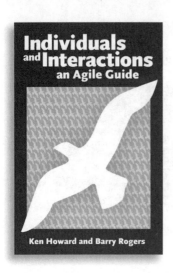

FREE Online Edition

Your purchase of *Individuals and Interactions: An Agile Guide* includes access to a free online edition for 45 days through the Safari Books Online subscription service. Nearly every Addison-Wesley Professional book is available online through Safari Books Online, along with more than 5,000 other technical books and videos from publishers such as Cisco Press, Exam Cram, IBM Press, O'Reilly, Prentice Hall, Que, and Sams.

SAFARI BOOKS ONLINE allows you to search for a specific answer, cut and paste code, download chapters, and stay current with emerging technologies.

Activate your FREE Online Edition at www.informit.com/safarifree

> **STEP 1:** Enter the coupon code: XQOZWWA.

> **STEP 2:** New Safari users, complete the brief registration form. Safari subscribers, just log in.

If you have difficulty registering on Safari or accessing the online edition, please e-mail customer-service@safaribooksonline.com